Woodcarver's Guide to
Sharpening, Tools
and
Setting Up Shop

Woodcarver's Guide to
Sharpening, Tools
and
Setting Up Shop

The Best of Woodcarving Illustrated Magazine

From the Editors of
Woodcarving Illustrated

FOX CHAPEL
PUBLISHING

© 2010 by Fox Chapel Publishing Company, Inc.

Woodcarver's Guide to Sharpening, Tools and Setting Up Shop is an original work, first published in 2010 by Fox Chapel Publishing Company, Inc. The patterns contained herein are copyrighted by the authors. Readers may make copies of these patterns for personal use. The patterns themselves, however, are not to be duplicated for resale or distribution under any circumstances. Any such copying is a violation of copyright law.

ISBN 978-1-56523-475-8

Library of Congress Cataloging-in-Publication Data

Woodcarver's guide to sharpening, tools and setting up shop / from the editors of Woodcarving Illustrated.
    p. cm. -- (The best of Woodcarving illustrated)

Includes index.

ISBN: 978-1-56523-475-8

1. Woodworking tools. 2. Wood-carving--Equipment and supplies. 3. Sharpening of tools. I. Woodcarving illustrated

TT186.W58 2010
684'.08--dc22

2009053463

To learn more about the other great books from Fox Chapel Publishing, or to find a retailer near you, call toll-free 800-457-9112 or visit us at *www.FoxChapelPublishing.com*.

Note to Authors: We are always looking for talented authors to write new books in our area of woodworking, design, and related crafts. Please send a brief letter describing your idea to Acquisition Editor, 1970 Broad Street, East Petersburg, PA 17520.

Printed in China
First printing: May 2010

Table
of Contents

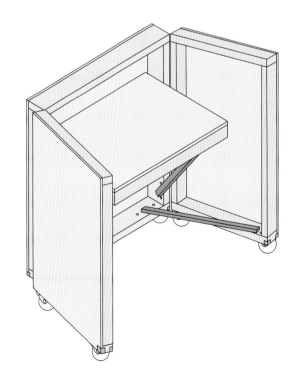

Introduction

Woodcarving Illustrated magazine presents this collection of some of our best shop-tested tips and techniques from expert carvers and inventive readers. Featured on the following pages are tips, techniques, projects, and ideas for everything from setting up shop to sharpening.

The first section, *Organizing Your Shop*, contains a plethora of information not only on setting up an effective workspace but also on carving safely, creating holders for all of your tools and materials, making the right workbench or board for your type of carving, and creating that all-important dust collector.

Reader Tip Boxes

Tips from readers of *Woodcarving Illustrated* are scattered throughout the book. Check them out to get in on creative solutions to common (and not-so-common) carving problems, such as creating a laptop chip collector from a carving apron (page 27), a stay-tight blade cover (page 73), and more!

Common Workshop Items, the second section, gives you information and ideas for some items you're likely to have around your shop. You'll learn tips and techniques for the basics of glues and sandpaper, the ins and outs of clamps and other holding devices, and more.

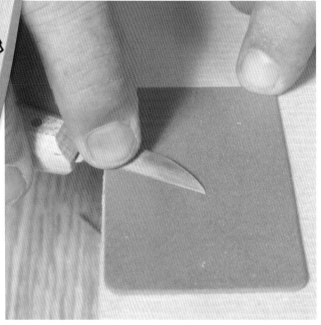

The third section, *Tools*, contains information on the different types of carving knives, but it also helps you navigate V-tools, mallets, files, rasps, rifflers, drawknives, spokeshaves, scorps, and punches. There's also information on customizing and making your own carving tools.

Sharpening is next with tips and techniques to help you tune up your sharpening skills. You'll come out of this section with a basic knowledge of sharpening and more details on this often-elusive aspect of carving.

So, grab your tools and get ready for some ideas and techniques that you're bound to want to dive into.

Finishing, the final section, rounds out the book with ideas on the steps you take once the carving is complete. Everything from setting up a finishing station to choosing a brush to working with finishes is covered here.

Organizing
Your Shop

The following pages contain a wealth of ideas and projects for organizing your shop. Read on for creative tips and tricks to solve those pesky problems in your woodshop. Create a workbench or carver's lapboard that's just right for you, or build your own affordable dust collector. There are even instructions to make clamps and carving vises. You're bound to find the answers to your organization woes here.

Build Your Own Carving Stand, by Jim Farley, page 28.

Carving
for Safety's Sake

Readers frequently send us suggestions about safe practices and accessories that are useful to prevent accidents while carving. We agree that safety should be everyone's concern. The editorial staff at WCI has put together ten tips to keep in mind:

1. Keep your tools sharp. Dull tools tend to be forced through the wood. When that happens, control is lost and accidents occur. Strive to develop razor-sharp edges so you are in control, not the tool.

2. When making dust or using chemicals, protect your eyes, nose, mouth, and skin. Some dusts cause eye irritations, and a number are potentially cancer causing when taken into the lungs over a prolonged period of time. Goggles and dust masks are essential when power carving and power sanding. Be aware that some woods are chemically treated and these may cause skin allergies as well as eye and respiratory problems. Avoid toxic solvents when possible. If you must use them, protect your skin, which will absorb the solvents, and your nose, which carries the damaging fumes to your lungs.

3. When running machines that produce high decibels, protect your ears. Hearing loss often accompanies prolonged exposure to noise. The loss is rarely reversible.

4. Properly dispose of rags used to apply oil finishes. Some oils used for finishes are susceptible to spontaneous combustion. These include tung, linseed, and cooking oils. Oily rags are best stored in an airtight metal container until they are disposed of. They should be soaked in water before they are put into the trash.

5. Don't carve when tired, distracted, or under stress. Surveys show most wood-related accidents occur when a person is fatigued or has his mind elsewhere. Stay alert and safe from mishaps. Carving can be relaxing, but the benefits are diminished when the mind is not alert.

6. Read the instructions that come with power tools. Cautions, precautions, and safety tips are frequently spelled out in a power tool manual. Accept the advice of the experts who design and work with the tools.

7. Protect your hands. Cut-resistant gloves and tape are available to carvers. Using them will help you avoid painful accidents when holding hand tools. Another tip: don't substitute a palm for a mallet. There is no ergonomic advantage to pounding a tool's end with your hand. Carpel tunnel syndrome, repetitive strain injury, and tennis elbow may result, and damage can be permanent.

8. Wear eye protection when power sharpening or using power tools. Safety glasses, face shields, and goggles are all available to protect your eyes. Don't subject your eyes to flying wood chips, dust, and metal shavings.

9. Make sure your woodcarving is securely clamped or held down whenever possible. A multitude of clamps and hold-downs that include bar, cam, quick-release, and web varieties are available to secure your work. Unless you are practiced at holding the wood in your protected hands when carving, look for a clamp to keep your work steady.

10. Take lessons from the experts. Many professional carvers offer instruction. Besides knowing how to efficiently remove wood, most have mastered carving styles incorporating safe techniques.

Setting
Up Shop

By Roger Schroeder

Ed Legg

In less time than it takes to carve a three-sided chip, you'll appreciate the three key words that keep the shops of wildfowl carver Ed Legg and master wood sculptor Ernest Szentgyorgyi productive: organization, organization, organization. They understand it's important not only to make the best use of their tools, but also to locate them quickly and work safely with them.

Both carvers graciously welcomed me into their shops to bring you the inside scoop on layout and tool use. Needless to say, I went back to my own work environment and made a few changes.

I'm sure the accompanying photos and captions will motivate you to make some improvements to your shop. I picked up invaluable ideas and tips from Ed and Ernest, on topics ranging from clutter and dust control to workbenches, heavy-duty woodworking equipment, and tool storage.

Ed's workspace is L-shaped and situated in one corner of a finished basement. An efficient floor plan helps him get birds roughed out and finished without disrupting the rest of the house. You can't help but conjure up images of a cockpit. Imagine Ed as the pilot, sitting on a rolling desk chair instead of a padded captain's seat, in a "cabin" where altimeters and control yokes have been replaced by grinders, bits, woodburners, airbrushes, and reference materials.

In a work area measuring 7' by 7', with just about every foot given over to tools, cabinets, and work surfaces, Ed seems to have it all within an arm's reach. Two flexible shaft machines hang to one side of the bench, and two micro motor tools take up a corner of the worktable. Why

Ed Legg

A cabinet with narrow shelves mounted on Ed's workbench helps organize a myriad of tools and accessories.

Paint tubes are mounted on the outside of the cabinet doors.

Brushes are stored on the inside of a cabinet door.

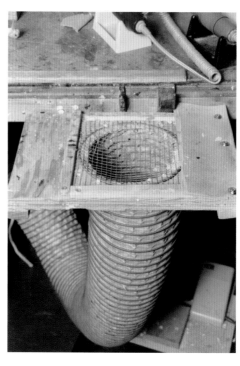

The hose and framework of Ed's homemade dust collector is movable.

pairs of rotary tools? Pointing to a set of high-speed pieces of equipment, Ed explains that one machine has a collet for ⅛" bits, the other accepts ³⁄₃₂" bits. Time spent changing collets is time lost carving birds, he reasons.

Many workbenches seem to cater to chaos, but Ed's, while crammed with tools and accessories, is as neat as a Swiss watchmaker's worktable. The bench, made from plywood covered with Masonite and measuring 36" by 78", is unpretentious as benches go, but it's definitely the center of action. Grinding bits stand upright in wood blocks. Burning pens do the same, suggesting soldiers in military rows. And when small accessories start to accumulate and bring about disarray, Ed arranges them where they won't

get misplaced on a magnetic bar mounted on what looks like a miniature sawhorse.

Not to let any cabinet space go unused, Ed mounts his brushes on the inside of one cabinet door, free from dust and mishandling. So the outside of another cabinet isn't underutilized, he places his paint tubes in racks attached to the faces of the plywood doors. Ed prefers having his paint inventory clearly visible, not stored in boxes or drawers. When setting up his shop, Ed figured on having as many cabinets as possible. In one, situated behind where he keeps his drafting table, he stows his references, including painting notes, patterns, and bird photos. Much of the material is organized in loose-leaf notebooks. Ed even has

Ed's airbrush box.

Shop facts

Ed Legg
- Primary shop square footage: 49
- Size of major workbench: 36" by 78"
- Output each year: two major wildfowl carvings and 25 smaller birds

Ernest Szentgyorgyi
- Primary shop square footage: 672
- Size of major workbench: 39" by 96"
- Output each year: numerous carved moldings, cabinets, mantles, figures

an inventory book that helps him locate a particular tool or accessory by drawer, shelf, or cabinet.

If Ed can't buy it in a catalog, he designs and makes what he needs. Because he likes to mask off areas of a bird when airbrushing, he wants both hands free. While he could mount the bird on a dowel, Ed decided to construct an open box measuring approximately 11" high by 8" wide. The device holds the bird securely while giving Ed access to the belly and other hard-to-reach areas. Softened with carpet padding, the box attaches to the front of his workbench. Once in place, Ed can work with both hands and move the bird with ease.

Key to dust control is a dust collector positioned at the front of the workbench. Commercially made in-lap systems cost $300 or more. Ed's homemade dust collector cost less than $50. After purchasing a Dayton 500 CFM

Ed's miniature sandpiper was the subject of a two-part article in *Woodcarving Illustrated's* Issues 24 and 25.

Floor Plan – Ed Legg's Workshop

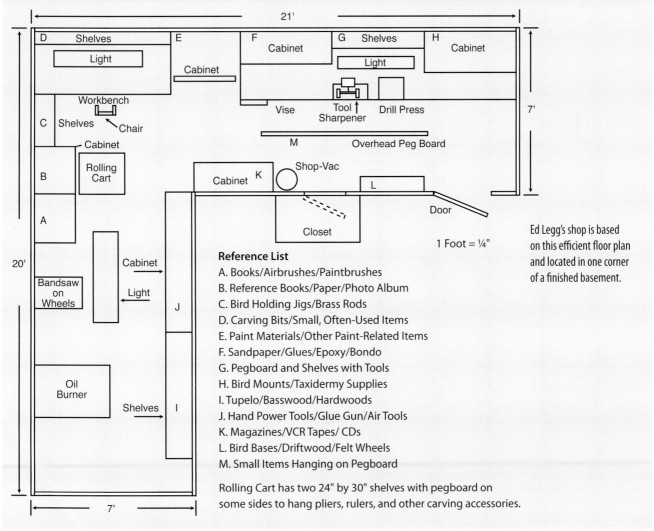

Reference List
A. Books/Airbrushes/Paintbrushes
B. Reference Books/Paper/Photo Album
C. Bird Holding Jigs/Brass Rods
D. Carving Bits/Small, Often-Used Items
E. Paint Materials/Other Paint-Related Items
F. Sandpaper/Glues/Epoxy/Bondo
G. Pegboard and Shelves with Tools
H. Bird Mounts/Taxidermy Supplies
I. Tupelo/Basswood/Hardwoods
J. Hand Power Tools/Glue Gun/Air Tools
K. Magazines/VCR Tapes/ CDs
L. Bird Bases/Driftwood/Felt Wheels
M. Small Items Hanging on Pegboard

Rolling Cart has two 24" by 30" shelves with pegboard on some sides to hang pliers, rulers, and other carving accessories.

Ed Legg's shop is based on this efficient floor plan and located in one corner of a finished basement.

1 Foot = ¼"

motor, he attached a piece of discarded hose. Then, he made a "catcher" framework covered with chicken wire, and his wife sewed together the dust and chips collection bag. There's enough hose, Ed points out, that the framework can be moved to fit under his band saw, the only large piece of woodworking equipment in the shop. The band saw is on wheels so it can be moved about and ultimately out of the way.

Also on wheels is a small drafting table measuring 25" by 30". On its surface Ed can lay out reference material, patterns, and drawing tools. Not to let any space go to waste, Ed hangs his magnifier, pliers, and leather strops underneath the table.

A mobile drafting table supplements Ed's primary workbench.

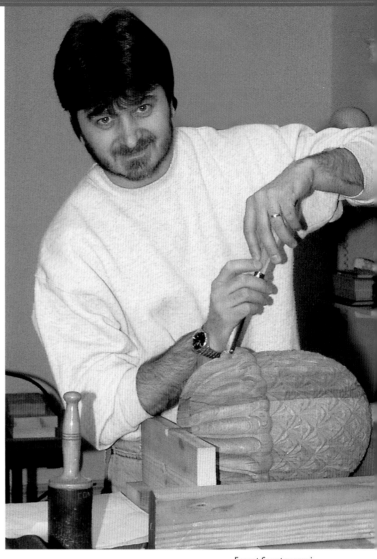

Ernest Szentgyorgyi

Ernest Szentgyorgyi

Ernest's shop, which he calls the "operating room" and which takes up the basement of his home, is minimalist compared to Ed's. While a band saw and table saw are present, a fair percentage of the space is occupied by a simple workbench and worktable. Ernest's vision is to have plenty of room to carve, with the emphasis on hand tools, not power tools. For showing off his work, as well as having a place to illustrate his projects for clients, Ernest recently built a design room with nearly the same square footage as his workshop.

Ernest uses a hydraulic post lift table to support his oak workbench top. He says the ideal bench is adjustable in height like his. "You need to feel comfortable with it so that carving is not tiring and backbreaking," he explains. The steel stand has a flat surface measuring 24" by 36" and is

A hydraulic post lift table is used to adjust the height of Ernest's workbench.

Ernest secures a project in a bar clamp, which is held in a machinist's vise.

Detail of Ernest's walnut headboard.

supported by four heavy-duty corner posts. The height, which adjusts from 30½" to 48", is raised and lowered with a hand crank. A floor lock, which keeps the table in place, is foot operated. The laminated oak bench top Ernest bolted to the stand measures an impressive 2" thick by 39" wide by 8' long because he does not want to limit himself to small projects. If Ernest needs to spread out a large design or support a lengthy piece of lumber, the 26-square-foot work surface makes that possible. Even how he positions the bench is important. Although the wheeled stand allows him to move the workbench easily, Ernest wants to be able to walk around it. He stations the bench in the middle of his shop, with plenty of space on all sides.

Ernest not only needs to make the best use of the tools but also has to locate them quickly. If he purchases a tool with a round handle, he immediately replaces the handle with a hexagonal one. Chisels and gouges need to remain stationary, he states. Six-sided handles stay in place and won't roll around on the workbench. While looking at the rows of tools Ernest has lined up on his workbench, sharpened edges pointing away from him because he was taught to do it that way, he notes that every tool has its place. When he picks up a carving tool, he puts it back in the same position and location. "I don't want to risk losing time looking for a tool," he says.

Ernest prefers to use a bar clamp to hold a small figure. While the bar clamp might seem more at home in a cabinetmaker's shop, he says it not only accommodates a range of figure heights, but also lets him release the carving with a twist or two of the turn handle. Once the jaws are loosened, he can rotate the wood to different

Ernest owns nearly 500 American- and European-made gouges, V-tools, and chisels.

A toggle clamp in action.

positions or even turn the piece 180°. Holding the bar clamp in a heavy-duty machinist's vise allows him to rotate the clamp itself.

When working on small panels for relief carvings, Ernest uses toggle clamps. One commission had him working on a series of identical decorative relief panels. Each panel was held in place by the rubber ends of in-line clamps. Unlike the horizontal and vertical toggle clamps available, in-line clamps put pressure on the edge of the wood, not on the top surface. As a result, these clamps do not interfere with the carving tools or the pattern.

Cutting Triangular Blanks

It can be difficult to cut triangular blanks for some projects using a table saw or band saw with a traditional rip fence. Because I planned to cut several, I designed a jig that makes it safe and easy to cut a 1⅜" wide x 1⅜" thick block diagonally into two triangular pieces on a band saw. This jig was designed for my Sears band saw; the base is sized to fit from one side of the table to the other.

Cut a slot halfway through the base in the center of the blank to accommodate the band saw blade. Cut two 45° grooves on each of the upright pieces, creating a triangle to hold the corners of the stock. Set your table saw at a 45° angle and cut one side of the groove. The cut should be half the thickness of the wood you are using for the uprights. Flip the blank over and cut the other side of the groove. Screw the uprights to the base so the distance from the bottom of one groove to the bottom of the opposite groove is 1⅞". Adjust the space as necessary to fit the stock you are cutting. Leave a bit of space to allow the blank to be pushed through the jig.

To use the jig, position it on your band saw table with the blade centered in the jig. Clamp the jig in place and feed the blanks through. Push the blank through the jig until you get close to the blade. Then, feed the next blank through. The incoming blank pushes the first blank through the blade. On the last blank, pull the wood past the saw blade from the cut side.

Don Worley
New Carlisle, OH

A simple jig makes it safe and easy to cut triangular blanks for a variety of carvings.

Tool
Holder

By Lynn Diel

Lynn Diel's folding tool holder protects sharp edges and can be built with a minimum of parts.

Almost every carver I meet has a way to organize tools for home use, for bringing to club meetings, or for taking on trips. Tool rolls, boxes, and even fancy tool chests all come into play. After using these various tool totes, I decided to design my own. Organization was certainly a criterion, but I also needed to keep the carving tools separated and consequently sharp. My design holds 12 tools or craft supplies, such as paintbrushes, but it can be made larger to accommodate more. It folds for easier storage, and when open, all the tools are lined up and readily accessible. When I added the cost of the components, I found the tool holder cost about $4.50.

Construction

The basic design of the tool holder has lengths of plastic pipe fitted top and bottom into wood (see **Figure 1**). Start with a piece of hardwood lumber measuring at least 39". Most home centers carry 1x2 boards (actual size ¾" by 1½"), so ripping the lumber will not be necessary. A 4' length of poplar costs around $2.

Schedule 20 plastic water pipe has an outside diameter of 1" and an inside diameter of .92". It is available at many home improvement centers or from local plumbing supply shops. The project requires a dozen 3½"-long sections of pipe, so you will need a length measuring at least 4'. Give yourself some extra pipe to allow for saw kerfs and a mis-cut or two. Since the plastic pipe is sold in 10' lengths, you may want to build two tool holders.

Cut the lumber into four equal-size boards and locate a centerline through the length of each (see **Figure 2**). Locate the centers for the dozen sections of plastic pipe and, using a 1⅛" Forstner bit, drill the holes ½" deep. A

Two Bit Organizers

These two holders for bits will help you further organize your tools and work area.

Recycled CD Case Bit Holder

A container that once stored blank CDs works great to hold power carving burs. The containers are stackable, and you can store a lot in a small area with them. Use the clear plastic disc that protects the blank CDs as a template to draw the size of the holder onto a piece of Styrofoam or wood. I prefer Styrofoam because you just push the burs into the foam. If you use wood, you need to drill holes to match the different sizes of the bur shanks.

If you position the burs to the outside of the first Styrofoam ring, you can add a smaller disc on top of the larger one. That way, all the burs will be visible. The plastic cover protects the burs from falling out and getting lost. Use larger CD holders to store mini carving tools.

Leon Hall
Meriden, CT

Refrigerator Magnet Bit Holder

Tired of searching for the rotary carving bit that just rolled off your carving bench? To prevent this from happening, tape an advertisement refrigerator magnet—the flat, flexible ones from the plumber, lawyer, or dentist—to your bench top. When you remove the burr from the chuck, place it on the magnetic pad. It'll stay right where you want it.

This magnet is also useful any time you are working with small screws or other metal parts. If you don't have any extra magnets, you can get magnetic sheets at the craft store.

Michael Kutch
Bath, PA

A refrigerator magnet keeps bits where you put them.

drill press is more accurate than a handheld power drill. Take two of the boards and drill pilot holes ⅛" in diameter straight through.

Use the holes left by the point of the Forstner bit as a guide. Turn the boards over and drill holes using a 1" Forstner bit, making sure to break through to the 1⅛" holes drilled from the opposite side. The two different-size holes provide the opening for the tool and allow the pipe to seat itself so it does not come all the way through the board (see **Figure 3**).

To assemble, spread a thin layer of slow-setting epoxy over the outside of the bottom ¼" of each length of pipe.

Press each piece into the bottom board. Set the assembly on the work surface and spread epoxy on the outside of the top ¼" of the pipes. Starting at one end, press the top board down on the pipes. If the epoxy runs out of the holes, use denatured alcohol for cleanup. Put aside the assembly for overnight drying.

To join the pair of tool holders together, line them up and clamp. Make sure the hinges, which are available at home centers and craft stores, are on the ends that have extra wood so the screws do not come in contact with the pipes. Screw the hinges in place, and the holder is ready to organize your tools at home or on the road.

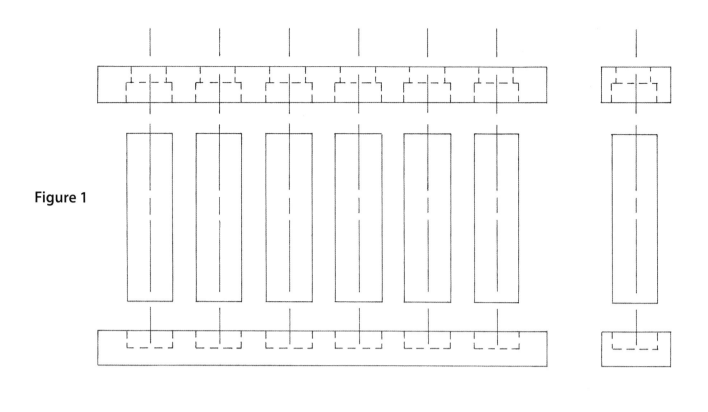

Figure 1

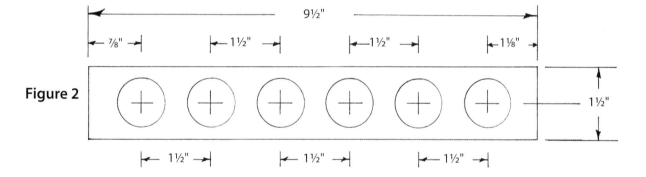

Figure 2

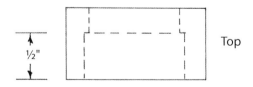

Top

Bottom

Figure 3

Materials & Tools

Materials:
- 4 each ¾" thick x 1½" wide x 9½" long hardwood
- 12 each 3½"-long sections of 1" schedule 20 plastic water pipe
- 2 each ¾" wide x ¾" long brass hinges

Tools:
- Hacksaw
- Drill press
- 1" and 1⅛" Forstner bits
- ⅛" diameter drill bit

Portable
Carving Station

By James M. Haumesser

If you're like me, space for a workbench is at a premium. I designed this portable workbench that gives me ample space for carving and painting. When closed, it takes up less room than a folded Ping-Pong table.

The basic unit is made from a 48" x 48" piece of ½" plywood, glued and attached to a 2x6 wooden frame. The doorframes are made from 2x4 lumber. The doors are 24" x 48", which will use up the other half of the 4' x 8' sheet of plywood.

By having multiple holes at the base, the angle of the doors can be either narrow or fairly wide. You can add an optional piece of plywood, hinged to the top, with cutouts to allow a standard box fan to fit on top. By attaching a 20" x 20" filter to the fan, it will collect most of the overspray during painting.

I also added several small lights and a couple of outlets. The unit has the outlets wired to a switch and has about 15' of cord. This lets me turn off everything from one place when I leave the bench for short breaks.

Step 1: Cut all of the pieces. Use the dimensions listed in the materials list.

Step 2: Drill the holes for the door spreaders. These are on the door bottom stock and the base unit bottom stock. Drill the holes for the table supports on the inside of the base unit side stock.

Step 3: Assemble the base unit frame. Glue and nail or screw the 2x6 frame together.

Step 4: Attach the plywood to the base frame.

Step 5: Assemble the doorframes. Glue and nail or screw the 2x4 frames together.

Step 6: Attach the plywood to the doorframes.

Step 7: Attach the doors to the base. Use 1"-wide piano hinges that run the length of the doors.

Step 8: Assemble the folding carving table frame. Glue and nail or screw the 1x2 frame together.

Step 9: Cover the table frame with plywood. Attach the table to the base unit with door hinges.

Step 10: Assemble the door spreaders. Drill ½"-diameter holes on each end of the 1x2 stock. Add the ½" diameter x 1½" long bolts to either end. These spreaders keep the doors open while you carve.

Step 11: Assemble the table supports. Drill a ¼"-diameter hole in the bottom end of both 1x2 table supports. Glue a ¼"-diameter dowel in place and position it in the top table support hole (in the side of the base unit frame). Prop the table up so it is horizontal and mark the location for the top dowel in the 1x2 table support. Trim the support to size, and drill and attach a ¼"-diameter dowel on the side and end opposite the first dowel.

Step 12: Attach six swivel chair casters to the bottom of the workbench. Mount one caster to each end of the base unit and one on either end of both doors. Add 1"-wide metal corner braces at each of the bottom corners near the casters to reinforce the wood.

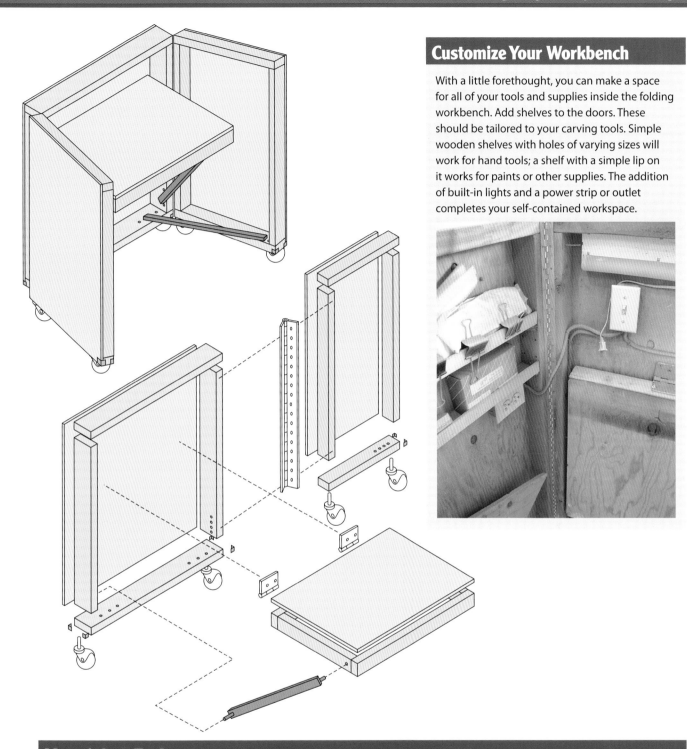

Customize Your Workbench

With a little forethought, you can make a space for all of your tools and supplies inside the folding workbench. Add shelves to the doors. These should be tailored to your carving tools. Simple wooden shelves with holes of varying sizes will work for hand tools; a shelf with a simple lip on it works for paints or other supplies. The addition of built-in lights and a power strip or outlet completes your self-contained workspace.

Materials & Tools

Materials:
- 4 each 2" x 4" x 24" studs (door top & bottom)
- 4 each 2" x 4" x 45" studs (door sides)
- 2 each 2" x 6" x 48" studs (base unit top & bottom)
- 2 each 2" x 6" x 45" studs (base unit sides)
- 2 each ½" x 24" x 48" plywood (door sheathing)
- 2 each 1" x 2" x 24" studs (table sides)
- 2 each 1" x 2" x 43" stud (table front & back)

- 2 each 1" x 2" x 22" (door supports)
- 2 each 1" x 2" x 38" (table supports)
- ½" x 48" x 48" plywood (base unit sheathing)
- ½" x 27" x 43" plywood (folding table top)
- 6 swivel chair casters
- 2 each 1" x 48" piano hinges
- 2 standard door hinges
- 4 each ¼" x 1½" long dowels
- 4 each ½" x 1½" long bolts

- 8 each 1" metal corner braces
- Wood glue of choice
- Assorted nails or screws

Tools:
- Saw of choice (to cut lumber to size)
- Screwdriver or hammer
- Drill with ¼"- and ½"-diameter drill bits

Relief
Carver's Workbench

By Vernon DePauw
Jerseyville, IL

I am a relief carver who started out using the kitchen table as a workbench. However, I soon found myself wanting a carving bench. Unfortunately, the cost of benches I found in catalogs was a deterrent, and I was not happy with their designs. One day, while looking through a carving magazine from the 1970s, I saw a carving bench and immediately thought of a piece of mahogany I had found in an old warehouse. It was wood I wanted to carve, but small nail holes and imbedded sand particles made it unsuitable. This was also about the time I started demonstrating woodcarving at historical events. I decided to make a bench that would be easy to move around and have the look of an earlier time period.

My salvaged mahogany top measures 2" thick x 23" long x 18" wide. With those dimensions as the basis for the framework, I designed the rest of the bench using scrap 2x4s. The only items I purchased were the carriage bolts that hold the lumber together and two holdfasts, which cost $7 each. I even made the wooden mallet I use to tighten the holdfasts. The bench top tilts up or lies flat, and it has leg extensions, allowing me to stand or sit while I work at it.

I have been carving for nearly 30 years and have received many awards for my relief carvings. I exhibited four of my relief scenes in a Smithsonian Institute exhibit entitled "Barn Again." My mahogany top has come a long way from almost becoming a carving to being a substantial accessory to all of my relief work.

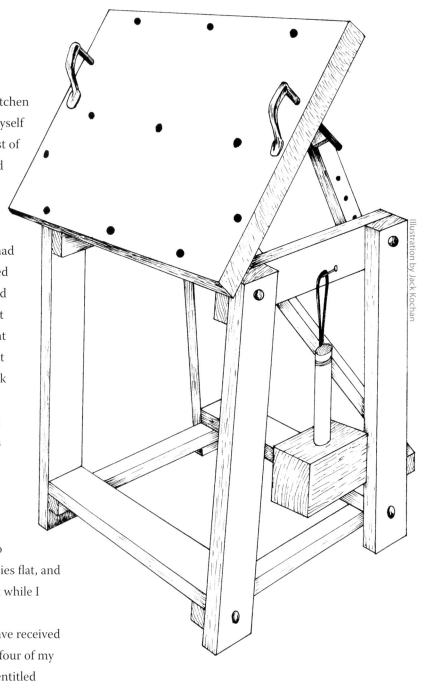

Illustration by Jack Kochan

One-Legged
Carving Bench

By Gene Carey
Cicero, NY

Volunteering to demonstrate woodcarving at a local show inspired me to create my one-legged carving bench. When I demonstrate woodcarving, the tables available are not sturdy enough for me to use my bench hooks, so I came up with this bench as a solution. I can place this small unit into the trunk of my car, set it up in a minute, and begin carving.

Making Your Bench

Only simple woodworking tools are needed to make this 8-pound bench. First, cut the shoulders on the leg to form a 1½" x 1½" tenon. (A tenon is a projection made on the end of one piece of wood that fits into a mortise on another piece, making a joint.) The shoulders of the tenon are located the same distance as the front of the chair (or 18").

Cut a square hole (mortise) in the bottom board to accept the tenon, 3" from one end. Screw and glue the seat extensions to the other end of the bottom board to provide a wider seat than the 2" thickness x 8" width it provides.

Next, assemble the bench as shown in the diagram. I put the bench together in about one hour with screws using an electric drill and a screwdriver bit. Don't forget to round off the sharp edges of the seat.

This bench weighs eight pounds and can be made with free scrap wood.

Using Your New Bench

To use this carving bench, slip the leg into the square hole in the bottom board. Support the other end of the bench on a chair, sit down and go to work.

I wedge my carving project between the cleats I mount on the top, allowing me to use a hand tool and mallet on the carving. Or, I can use just a hand tool in a push mode. By mounting a cleat on the side, I can cut sideways as well as from back to front.

Another way to mount the carving is to screw it down using a screw with machine threads on one half and wood screw threads on the other. The end with the wood threads is screwed into the carving wood. The other end goes through a hole drilled in the top and fastened with a nut.

A One-Legged Carving Bench

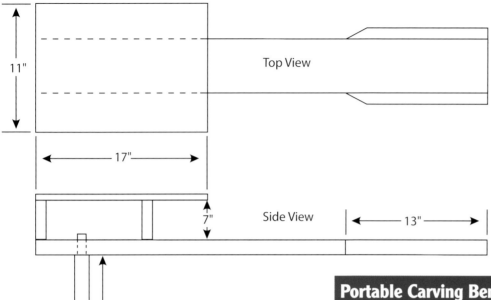

11"

17"

Top View

Side View

7"

13"

11"

End View

Portable Carving Bench

Here's another portable carving option. Because many carvers don't have space for a permanently mounted carving bench, a Workmate portable workbench is an ideal solution.

The top is split across its 30" width and accommodates a carver's box or bench hook. Bench-dog holes let you store tools or mount a carver's screw through the bench. You can also secure your work to the bench with a clamp.

One advantage to this setup is that you can move 360° around the bench to work on spots that would require you to reposition the workpiece on a permanent bench. It's sturdy enough to carve with a gouge and a mallet, and you can carve sitting or standing. When you're done carving, it packs up quickly.

Mike Tryba
Hotsprings, AR

Materials & Tools

Materials:
- 2" thick x 8" wide x 30" long (bottom)
- 2 each 2" thick x 8" wide x 7" long (risers)
- ¾" thick x 11" wide x 17" long plywood (top)
- 2" thick x 4" wide x 21" long (leg)
- 2" thick x 2" wide x 13" long (two seat extensions)

Tools:
- Wood screws
- Electric drill
- Screwdriver

Tabletop
Carving Bench and Magnifier

By Melvin Wheatley

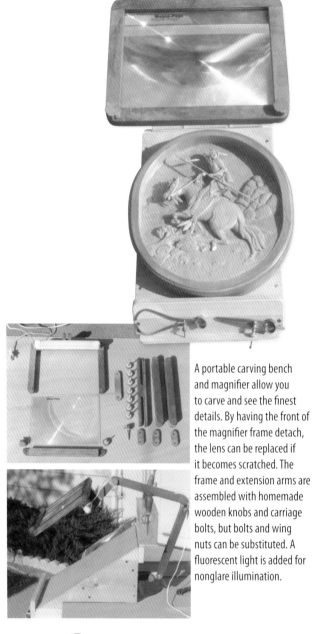

My back and shoulders started hurting when doing relief carving on a table at my carving club, so using scrap wood, I built a tilt-top carving bench adaptable to any tabletop.

My bench measures approximately 19½" x 12⅜" x 11¾". The sides and top were cut from a sheet of ¼" x 24" x 48" plywood and a ¾" x 1¼" x 19" pine board. Use screws to hold the components together and lengths of narrow pine as "ribs" or stiffeners inside the bench. The extension arms of the magnifier are mounted to ¾"-thick pine board and the frame for the magnifier is made from ¾"-thick pine or plywood.

The bench, which has a 30° tilt, accommodates relief carvings, woodburning, and wood engraving projects. The heavy-duty, full-page-size 2x magnifier, which can be purchased at any office supply store, is held in place by a frame with a removable front. Use knobs, T-slots, and carriage bolts to make the magnifier easy to remove. For more light, add a fluorescent light assembly. I mounted a clipboard to the side and added a tool holder to the top of the bench to make it more of a portable shop.

The total cost of materials—since I already had the wood—came to about $40.

A portable carving bench and magnifier allow you to carve and see the finest details. By having the front of the magnifier frame detach, the lens can be replaced if it becomes scratched. The frame and extension arms are assembled with homemade wooden knobs and carriage bolts, but bolts and wing nuts can be substituted. A fluorescent light is added for nonglare illumination.

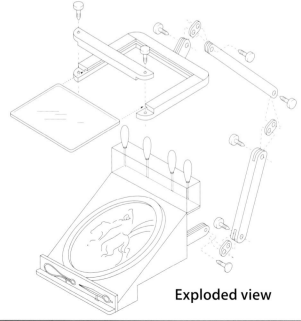

Exploded view

Carver's
Lapboard

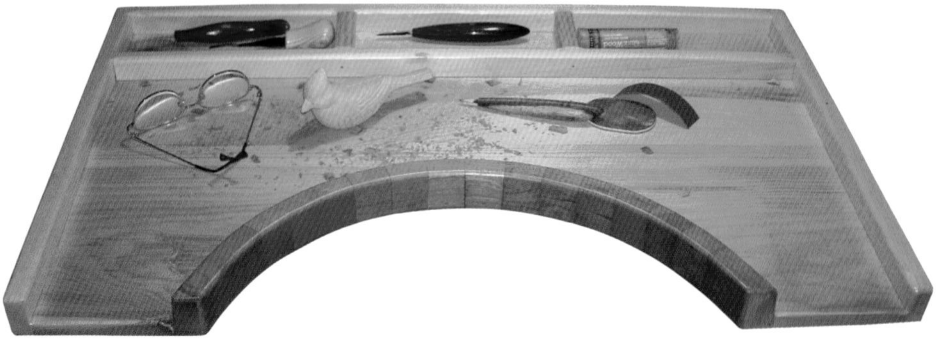

By Charles Brown

With this lapboard, you can carve mess-free anywhere—you can take your carving out of the basement and carve in the comforts of your easy chair. Flip it over, and it becomes a handy portable writing table. The dimensions of the lapboard depend on a couple of factors; I made mine to fit comfortably in my easy chair. Your physique and available materials also play a part in your dimensions.

Step 1: Cut out your keystone pieces. Set your table saw or miter saw to cut at a 5° angle. Make your first cut. Flip your piece end over end. Mark your piece so the long dimension will be 1¾" and make another cut. Continue cutting until you have 16 keystone pieces. I used several pieces of scrap; that way it keeps your hands away from the saw blade. Leave the two end pieces a little longer.

Step 2: Glue up the semicircle rail. Place these keystone pieces side-by-side. Flip them back and forth until they form the semicircle. The two long pieces will be your end pieces. Glue and clamp the pieces together, starting on one side. Work your way over to the other side. Allow the glue to dry, and sand it smooth.

Step 3: Assemble the lapboard bottom. Edge-glue the two pieces together. Trace the semicircle rail onto the bottom, and mark the end pieces of the rail. Cut out this semicircle with a scroll saw, band saw, or jigsaw and trim the ends of the rail to fit. Sand the cutout to fit the rail.

Step 4: Assemble the lapboard. Glue and nail the sides, back, and compartment to the bottom, as shown in the diagram. Glue and nail the semicircle rail in place. Trim the end pieces to match the bottom. Note: I left an opening to rest my arms on and to use as a cleanout. It is possible to add front pieces to completely enclose the lapboard. After assembly, I suggest you round over all edges for comfort.

Step 5: Apply your finish of choice. It is possible to leave it natural, but if you apply polyurethane, it will be easier to clean up.

Materials & Tools

Materials:
- 2 each ¾" x 9" x 28½" pine (bottom)
- 2 each ¾" x 1⅝" x 18" pine (side rails)
- 2 each ¾" x 1⅝" x 27" pine (back rail and front of compartments)
- 2 each ¾" x 1⅝" x 3" pine (compartment dividers)
- 2 each ¾" x 1⅝" x 15" hardwood of choice (see Step 1—keystone pieces)
- Wood glue of choice
- 8d finishing nails
- Assorted grits of sandpaper

Tools:
- Sander
- Jigsaw, band saw, or scroll saw
- Table saw or miter saw

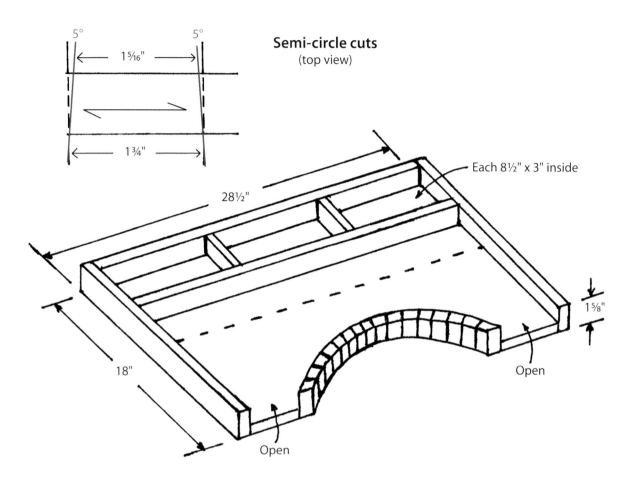

Semi-circle cuts
(top view)

5° 5°

1 5/16"

1 3/4"

28½"

Each 8½" x 3" inside

1 5/8"

18"

Open

Open

Laptop Chip Collector Makes Clean-up a Snap

Here's another way to capture chips and stay mess-free. With this homemade apron, the chips are collected in a handy pocket for quick and easy clean up! All it takes to make a carver's apron is a carpenter's nail apron, five binder clips, and a 24" piece of ¼"-diameter vinyl tubing.

Remove the stitching between the standard two pockets in the nail apron to make it into one large pocket. Starting in the center of the pocket, roll the seamed edge over the center of the tubing and lock it in place with a ¾" binder clip. Working out from the center, continue to fold the edge over the tubing and clamp it in place with the binder clips. Tuck the extra vinyl tubing down into the pocket to help keep it open.

When you're done carving, simply empty the chips from the pocket into the waste bin. Once you show your spouse how the apron works, he or she may let you carve in the living room! A few easy modifications turn a simple apron into a wood chip collector.

Donald Mertz
Wilmington, OH

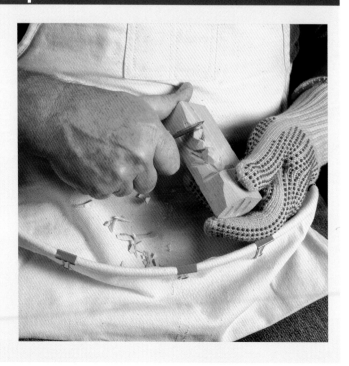

Build Your
Own Carving Stand

By Jim Farley

A proper carving stand makes it easy to maneuver your workpiece while providing the stability needed to make carving safe and enjoyable. Commercial holding devices are typically designed for smaller carvings and most are not capable of adjusting the vertical position of your work. This heavy-duty stand can handle anything from small caricatures to 20"-high busts and allows you to adjust the height of your carving to reduce fatigue and back strain.

Adjust the height to reduce fatigue and back strain.

Work attaches with a carver's screw for complete accessibility.

Sturdy table tilts a full 90°.

Quickly secures to your workbench with clamps or bench dogs.

The stand is simple to build and can be completed in a weekend. You can make the project using scrap wood, but I recommend using hardwood, because the stand will literally take a beating. For a minimal investment of 10 to 12 hours of your time and $50 in materials, you will have a sturdy workstation to make carving safer and more enjoyable for years to come. A comparable commercial stand costs about $500.

I was introduced to this style of carving stand when I took a carving class in Austria. I learned much about carving, but more about working with method and efficiency. I set out to make a benchtop carving stand for the Stubai carver's screw I bought in Austria. The resulting stand is adjustable in height and allows the table to be tilted 90°. The carving is attached to the table with a carver's screw and can easily be rotated, providing complete access to the carving. This holding method eliminates metal clamps that can nick the sharp tools.

Cut the materials to size as listed in the materials list. Both imperial and metric measurements are included. The center table support piece should fit tightly between the posts to eliminate movement of the table. With the stand clamped to your bench, you will have all of the advantages of a large stand in a compact easy-to-use unit.

Materials & Tools

Materials:

- 2 each ⅜" (10mm)-diameter threaded knobs (side handles)
- ⅜" (10mm)-diameter by 19⅝" (500mm)-long threaded rod (cut in half for the tightening rods)
- ⅜" (10mm)-diameter threaded insert for back handle
- Carver's screw
- 2" x 3" x 3" (51mm x 76mm x 76mm) hardwood of choice (screw block)
- 3 each ⅜" (10mm)-diameter washers
- ⅜" (10mm)-diameter nut
- Wooden shims or wedges (mortise wedges)
- #8 by 3" (76mm) wood screws

Base Unit:

- 1" x 10⅝" x 15¾" (25mm x 270mm x 400mm) hardwood of choice (base)
- 2 each 2½" x 3⅛" x 27½" (65mm x 70mm x 700mm) hardwood of choice (posts)
- 2 each 1" x 4⅜" x 10⅝" (25mm x 110mm x 270mm) hardwood of choice (side supports)

- 1¹⁄₁₆" x 1⅜" x 2½" (30mm x 35mm x 65mm) hardwood of choice (bottom spacer)
- 1⅜" x 2⅜" x 2½" (35mm x 60mm x 65mm) hardwood of choice (top spacer)
- ⁹⁄₁₆" x 2⅜" x 6⅞" (15mm x 60mm x 175mm) hardwood of choice (top support)
- 1³⁄₁₆" x 2⅜" x 6⅞" (20mm x 60mm x 175mm) hardwood of choice (carrying handle)

Table and Table Support:

- 11⅜" x 3⅛" x 5¹⁵⁄₁₆" (35mm x 80mm x 150mm) hardwood of choice (center table support)
- 2 each 1⅜" x 3⅛" x 7⅜" (35mm x 80mm x 195mm) hardwood of choice (inner table supports)
- 2 each 1¹⁄₁₆" x 2⅜" x 3⅛" (30mm x 60mm x 80mm) hardwood of choice (outer table supports)
- 1" x 2⅜" x 9½" (25mm x 60mm x 240mm) hardwood of choice (back handle)
- 1" x 9⅞" x 12⅝" (25mm x 250mm x 320mm) hardwood of choice (table)

- 2 each 1⅜" x 3⅛" x 5½" (35mm x 80mm x 140mm) hardwood of choice (outside table pivots)
- 1⅜" x 3⅛" x 3⅛" (35mm x 80mm x 80mm) hardwood of choice (center table pivot)
- 1" x 3⅛" x 6⅞" (25mm x 80mm x 175mm) hardwood of choice (back clamp)
- 1" x 1⅜" x 2¾" (25mm x 35mm x 70mm) hardwood of choice (nut cover)

Tools:

- Saw of choice
- Router with rabbet bit and round-nose bit
- Drill with assorted bits
- Countersink bit
- Screwdriver
- 9mm gimlet (optional)
- Assorted clamps
- Woodworking chisels

BUILD THE CARVING STAND

Mark the tenons. Use a square and a pencil to mark tenons on both posts. I make the tenons 1" (25mm) long by 2¼" (57mm) wide by 2⅝" (70mm) thick. Trace along the pencil lines with a knife to create a small groove. It is easier to line up your saw and chisel in this groove.

Cut the tenons. Cut the waste away with a backsaw and carpenter's chisels. Cut two slots in each tenon for the mortise wedges with a backsaw. Drill ⅛" (3mm)-diameter holes at the end of the mortise slots to prevent the wood from splitting when you insert the wedges.

Assemble the posts. Glue and clamp the top and bottom spacers in place between the posts. Make sure the shoulders on the tenons stay aligned. Cut the side supports. I cut a curve to provide support while allowing room for the table to be lowered.

Add the top support. Rout or cut a ⅜" (10mm) by 2⅜" (60mm) rabbet on the front of the top of the posts. Glue and screw the top support into this rabbet. The top support is an ideal place to personalize your stand with initials or a relief carving.

Mark the location of the mortises. Temporarily clamp the side supports to the posts and place the assembly in position over the base. Use the tenons to mark the location of the mortises on the base.

Cut the mortises. Drill out as much waste as possible with a Forstner bit. Clean up the mortises with a carpenter's chisel. The mortises run the whole way through the base. The bottom of the mortises angle out about 6° on the sides.

Dry fit the post and base assembly. Fit the post assembly into the base, clamp the side supports in place, and trace around the side supports. Remove the post assembly and supports and drill pilot holes for the screws within these lines down through the base. Then, drill up through the pilot holes from the bottom of the base with a countersink drill bit.

Glue post assembly to base. Apply glue to tenon edges and insert into mortises. Apply glue to side support bottom. Attach side supports to base with wood screws. Tap wedges into tenon slots to pull posts to base. After glue dries, trim wedges and tenons; remove glue squeeze-out. Screw side supports to posts.

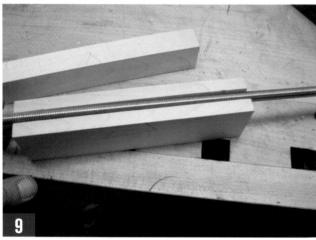

Cut channel for tightening rod. The center table support fits between posts and contains a threaded rod that adjusts the table height. Rip the top one-third off center support and cut a channel in center of bottom using router and round-nose bit. Make sure rod fits in channel, remove rod, glue/clamp center table support.

Prepare pivot parts. Use band saw or sander to round one corner on both inner table supports and center pivot. Round both bottom corners of outside pivots. This allows the table to swivel. Align all parts and mark location for pivot tightening rod (see Construction). Drill hole in each piece separately. Dry assemble.

Assemble the main table support. Lay the base on its back so the posts are flush with the work surface. Insert a ½" (13mm)-thick piece of scrap between the posts and place the center table support on top of the scrap. Position the inner table supports with the rounded corners facing up on either side of the center table support. Secure the assembly with clamps while you glue and screw the pieces together. Attach the outer table supports using the same method.

Make the nut cover. Use stock the same width as the center table support. Drill a hole for the threaded rod in the center of the nut cover. Position the nut over the hole and trace around the perimeter of the nut. Carve out the area inside the lines. Thread the nut on the end of the rod, place the nut cover over the nut, and insert the rod through the center table support. The nut cover must fit tightly between the inner table supports to keep the nut from turning.

Assemble the table pivots. Assemble the table supports and pivots using the pivot tightening rod. Use the assembly diagram to properly align the rounded corners on the pivots. Center the table horizontally on top of the assembly and mark the location of the table pivots on the bottom of the table. Drill two ½" (13mm) holes for the carver's screw. Center the holes horizontally and position them 2" (51mm) in from the front and back edges of the table.

Attach the table. Place a washer on both sides of the tightening rod and thread the side handles onto both ends. Tighten the handles to lock the table pivots in place. Drill pilot holes up through the table using the outlines of the pivots as a guide. Countersink the top of the holes. Position the table over the assembled table support and drill pilot holes down through the holes into the table pivots. Apply glue to the top of the table pivots and screw the table to the pivots.

Prepare the handles. Shape, glue, and screw the carrying handle to the top of the posts on the back of the unit. The shape of the handle is not important, but be sure to cut a recess to comfortably accommodate your fingers. Cut the back handle from scrap wood. Cut the sides of the handle at an angle to make it easier to turn. Drill a hole through the center of the back handle and attach a threaded insert that matches the threaded rod.

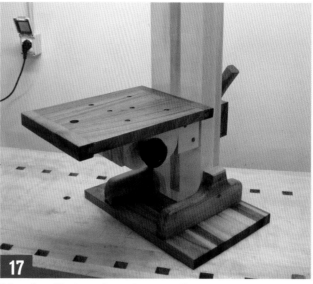

Prepare the back clamp and assemble the stand. Cut a ¼" (6mm)-deep by 2³⁄₁₆" (55mm)-wide rabbet on the ends of the back clamp. The raised area fits between the posts to keep the clamp from spinning. Drill a hole through the center of the back clamp. Insert the table through the posts and slide the back clamp in place. Slide a washer on the threaded rod and attach the back handle.

Adjust the table. Secure the stand to your workbench with clamps or bench dogs. Loosen the side handles underneath the tabletop, adjust the angle of the table, and tighten the handles to hold the table in place. To adjust the height of the table, loosen the back handle and lift or lower the table to the desired height. Tighten the back handle to lock in the table height.

Table Construction

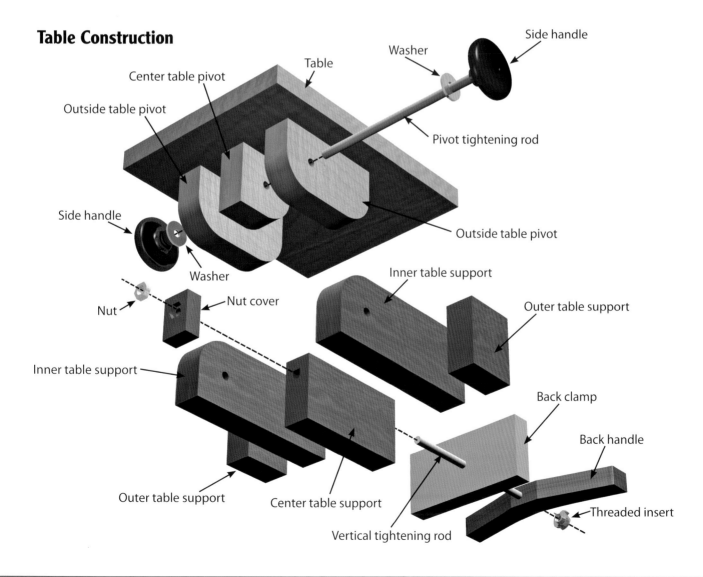

Center table pivot · Table · Washer · Side handle · Outside table pivot · Pivot tightening rod · Side handle · Washer · Nut · Nut cover · Outside table pivot · Inner table support · Outer table support · Inner table support · Back clamp · Back handle · Outer table support · Center table support · Vertical tightening rod · Threaded insert

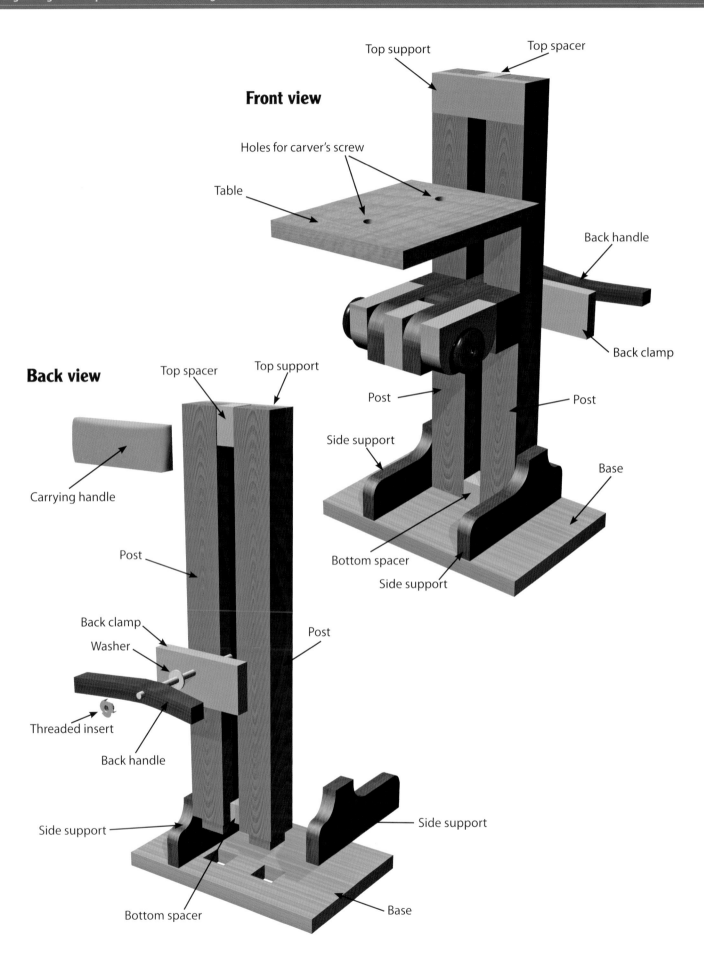

Front view

Top support

Top spacer

Holes for carver's screw

Table

Back handle

Back clamp

Post

Post

Side support

Base

Bottom spacer

Side support

Back view

Top spacer

Top support

Carrying handle

Post

Post

Back clamp

Washer

Threaded insert

Back handle

Side support

Side support

Bottom spacer

Base

USING A CARVER'S SCREW

1

Drill a hole in the carving. I use a ⁵⁄₁₆" (9mm) gimlet, but you can use a drill bit and drill. Center the hole in the bottom of the carving. Drill into the blank 1½" to 2" (38 to 51mm). Make sure you do not drill into an area that will be carved.

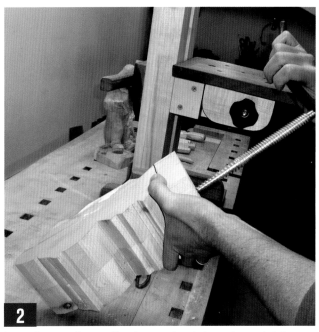

2

Insert the carver's screw. Use a box wrench or the integral square hole in the handle of the carver's screw to drive the tapered screw into the carving as far as possible.

3

Attach the carving to the table. Insert the carver's screw through the hole in the table. Drill a hole through the center of a 2" x 3" x 3" (51mm x 76mm x 76mm) block and slide the block over the exposed end of the screw. Slide the washer over the bottom of the screw and tighten up the handle until the carving is secure.

Why Use a Carver's Screw?

- A tapered carver's screw, such as the Stubai carver's screw, ensures that it is always tight, even after removing it and re-attaching it on the same sculpture.

- The hold on a vertical block of wood is exceptional, and there are no metal parts near your carving that can take a nick out of your sharp tools.

- A tap of your mallet on the wing nut will loosen the carving so you can rotate it, and another tap tightens things back up quickly.

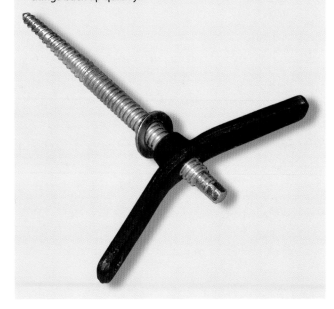

A simple benchtop vise holds a carving between adjustable jaws. An L-shaped hook engages the table, and a piece of wood placed underneath the vise elevates it for greater comfort and visibility.

Benchtop
Carving Vise

By Louis Foshay

Carvings often require a vise or holding fixture for safety and ease of removing wood. My benchtop carving vise allows me to remove large amounts of wood from a variety of projects. The fixture is especially invaluable when I have both hands busy with a mallet and chisel or gouge and the carving cannot be handheld.

Custom-Make Your Vise

The size of the vise I made measures approximately 12" wide x 15" long with jaws that are 1¼" square. These dimensions were chosen to accommodate the size of the carvings I typically work on. But a larger or smaller vise can easily be built to suit your carving needs. However, I do advise that the jaws open wide enough to hold a variety of carvings from very narrow to fairly wide. The drawings, then, provide assembly details rather than dimensions.

The vise consists of four major components: a base, a pair of jaws to hold the carving, a hook that holds the vise to a table or workbench, and a stop board that prevents the carving from shifting or moving out of the jaws. To hold the jaws to the base, four carriage bolts, flat washers, and wing nuts or hex nuts are required.

If you have, as I do, a selection of hardware around your home and some sizeable pieces of ¾"-thick plywood, plus some lengths of ¾"- to 1"-thick hardwood, the cost for the vise is zero. If you need to purchase the components from a home center or lumberyard, I estimate the cost for the vise will be under $20.

Construction Notes

The jaws, which consist of pieces of hardwood and plywood, are adjustable with slots in each jaw. The slots are easily made with a scroll saw, but a jigsaw with a fine blade will do almost as good a job. I find that ¼" x 20 x 2" long bolts in ⅜"-wide slots work best for a vise of almost any size. To attach the hardwood to the plywood, I recommend both screws and glue. To protect the details on your carving from the pressure of the jaws, I suggest you cut an old computer mouse pad to size and glue the pieces to the faces of the hardwood pieces. You can use softwood, such as pine, but if you are carving a harder material, the wood will eventually have to be replaced because of depressions and dents.

Golf Ball Carving Vise

Golf ball "pickups" sold at large retailers and golf shops work great to hold the round balls while you carve. The pickups are essentially large suction cups designed to be attached to a ¾"-diameter rod so you can grab a golf ball without bending over.

The suction is strong enough that you can carve away on the golf balls without worrying that it will roll around or slip in your hand. If you are holding the pickup in your hand, I suggest you wear a carving glove, but if you insert a dowel in the bottom of the cup, you can clamp it in a vise.

Stan Crossman
Salem, WV

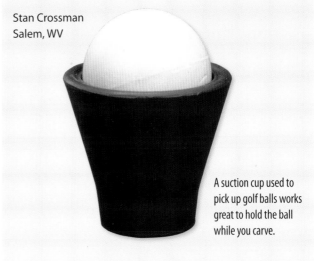

A suction cup used to pick up golf balls works great to hold the ball while you carve.

While the hook keeps the carving up close and prevents the vise from sliding away, the hook's opening may have play in it as mine does. If that's the case, you can wedge a piece of wood under the base at the rear of the vise. A bonus to the additional wood is the vise is elevated, providing great visibility. There is also less strain on the body if you have to lean over the carving for any length of time. If you find it comfortable working with the wedge, it can be mounted permanently with screws and glue.

Regardless of how big you make your benchtop carving vise, countersink all screws and make sure the carriage bolt heads are below the surface. The vise, which does not require a finish, can be put together in a few hours. Now, you have as part of your carving arsenal a tool that should last for years.

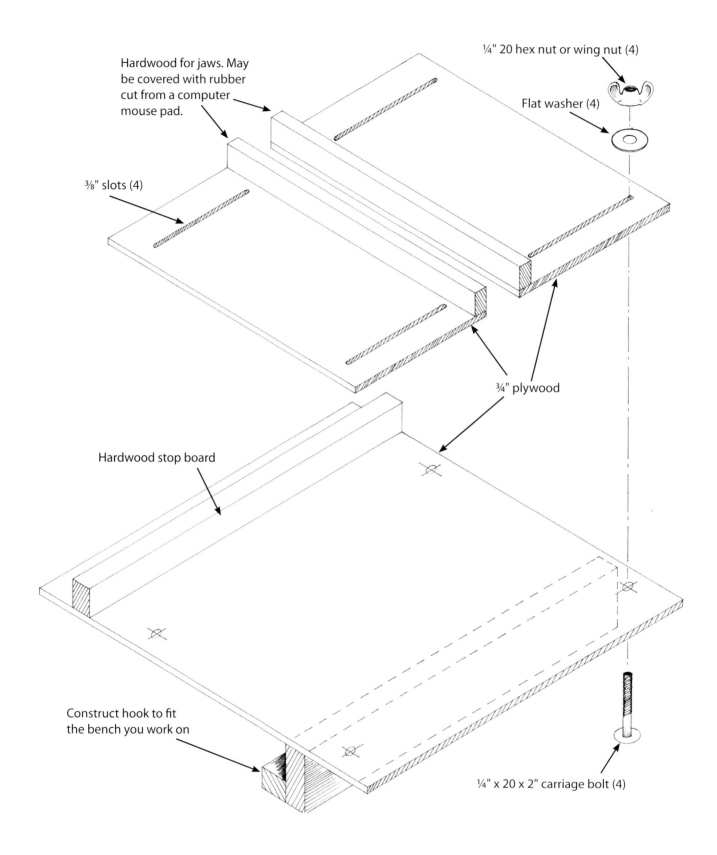

Hardwood for jaws. May be covered with rubber cut from a computer mouse pad.

¼" 20 hex nut or wing nut (4)

Flat washer (4)

⅜" slots (4)

¾" plywood

Hardwood stop board

Construct hook to fit the bench you work on

¼" x 20 x 2" carriage bolt (4)

Poor Man's
538 Model Easy-Hold Carver's Clamp

By Lynn Diel

After being diagnosed with carpal tunnel, a friend was afraid he would no longer be able to carve. His interest is in small projects that can be handheld as he shapes them. Discussing his options, he and I concluded carving was still feasible if a mechanical means for holding the wood were available. Expensive holding fixtures abound in the catalogs, but I came up with the vise clamp. A bar clamp holds the project while two other bar or C-clamps secure the vise to a work surface. For a permanent installation, the vise clamp can be bolted to a bench. The fixture, which cost only $5.38 in hardware (not counting the clamps), and took less than two hours to build, has proven to be helpful to my friend as well as to other carvers.

Step-By-Step Construction

The vise is constructed from craft-grade plywood. A 24" square by ¾" thick piece of birch plywood, big enough to accommodate all the wood parts, plus plenty of extra if you make a mistake cutting or drilling, costs around $6 at a home improvement center. If you have hardwood scraps available, they will work, too, although woods like poplar and maple are better choices than splintery species like oak. Poplar that is 1 x 4 (¾" by 3½") costs about $1 a linear foot at home improvement stores. You will need 4 feet for the project. Your local hardware store should have the necessary bolts, nuts, washers, screws, spacers, and knob.

Hardware Parts List:

Quantity	Description
6	¼" x 1½" carriage bolt
4	¼" washer
6	¼" nut
6	¼" fender washer
1	⅜" x 4" carriage bolt
2	½"-thick spacer with ⅜"-diameter hole
4	no. 8 1¼" flathead sheetrock or woodscrew
1	threaded knob

Step 1: Mark, cut, and drill the pivot blocks. After sawing the three 3"-wide pivot blocks and cutting them to their 5" lengths, locate the bolt holes by marking a point 1½" from the top and sides. Place the point of a compass at the bolt hole mark and draw a 1½" radius semicircle on all three blocks. Saw to shape with a band saw or scroll saw. Then, drill a 7⁄16"-diameter bolt hole in all three pivot blocks. If possible, stack the blocks and drill through all three at once.

Step 2: Add the two "wings" supporting the pivot blocks (see Figure 4**).** To ensure rigidity, each is attached to an outside pivot block with two 1¼" countersunk wood screws. See **Figure 1a** for their locations.

Step 3: Drill the holes and cut the slot for the center pivot block. The center pivot block requires two ¼" x 1½" carriage bolts, nuts, and fender washers to secure the bar clamp. See **Figure 1b** for the location of the holes, which can be 5⁄16" in diameter. Once the holes are drilled, saw out a slot for the bar clamp on the bottom of the center pivot block. This can be done on a table saw if you have a tenon jig, or on a band saw. The safest approach is to use a sharp handsaw and chisel. See **Figure 1c** for the dimensions of the slot.

Step 4: Cut a spacer block. For added stability between the two outside pivot blocks, and to prevent overstressing the woodscrews holding them to the wings, cut a spacer block to size. Make sure it is a snug fit. To hold it in place, use epoxy. See **Figure 2** for dimensions.

Step 5: Cut the wings to size and drill 1³⁄32" holes for ¼" x 1½" carriage bolts. Two bolts are required for each wing. See **Figure 3** for the size of the wings and the location of the bolt holes.

Step 6: Screw the outside pivot blocks to the wings. See **Figure 4** for assembly.

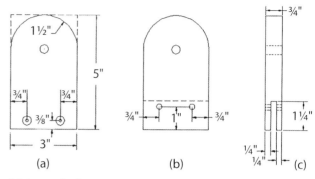

(a) Pivot Block Dimensions and Screw Hole Locations
(b) Center Pivot Block and Bolt Hole Locations
(c) Pivot Block Side View

Figure 1: Pivot Blocks

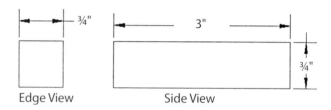

Edge View   Side View

Figure 2: Spacer Block

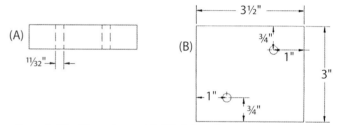

Figure 3: Wing Dimensions and Bolt Hole Locations

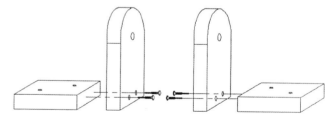

Figure 4: Assembly of Outside Pivot Blocks and Wings

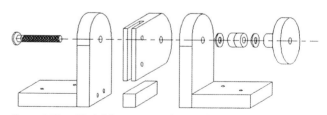

Figure 5: Pivot Block Adjustment Knob Assembly

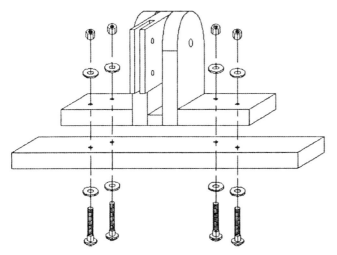

Figure 6: Assembly of Base and Wings

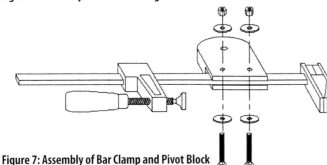

Figure 7: Assembly of Bar Clamp and Pivot Block

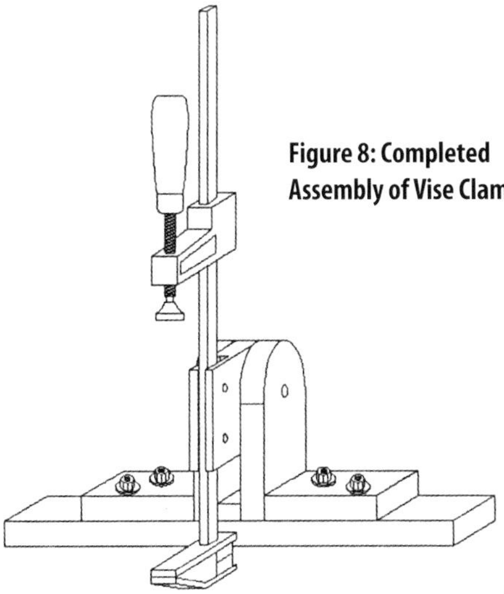

Figure 8: Completed Assembly of Vise Clamp

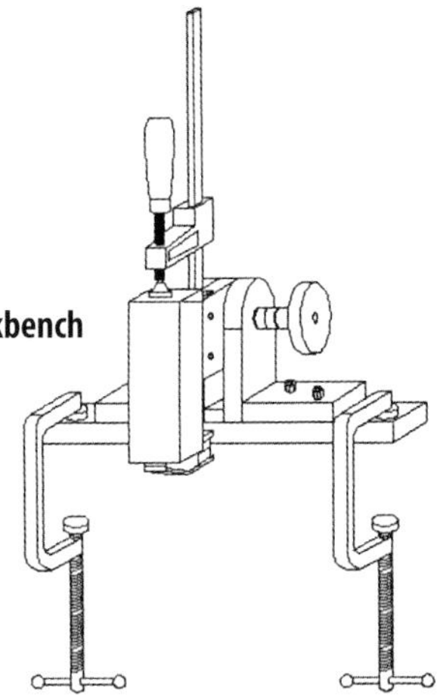

Figure 9: Vise Clamp Held to Workbench with C-Clamps or Bar Clamps

Step 7: Assemble the center pivot block. To enable the center pivot block to rotate, a ⅜" x 4" carriage bolt, two ½"-thick spacers with ⅜" holes, fender washers, and a threaded knob are needed. The knob chosen for the vise clamp is about 2¼" in diameter. See **Figure 5** for assembly. Don't forget to insert the spacer block.

Step 8: Cut the base to size. It should be at least 14" long to allow space for the wings and room for the clamps that secure it to a table or workbench. Locate and drill holes in the base for the ¼" x 1½" carriage bolts, nuts, and washers that secure the wings to the base. Make sure to countersink the bolt heads in the bottom of the base so they don't protrude and cause the vise to rock (see **Figure 6**).

Step 9: Once assembled, sand any rough edges. A finish is not required. Clamp or bolt the base to a bench. The size of the holding clamps will depend on the thickness of the bench or table, but they should be fairly heavy duty to prevent slippage. Fit a bar clamp—I recommend one that is 12" to 16" long—into the slot and tighten the bolts to make sure it is secure (see **Figures 7, 8,** and **9**).

Step 10: Add small blocks with protruding nails to attach to the clamps to secure a carving. A small dab of hot-melt glue will hold them in place. I also keep about 1" of space between the head of the tension screw and the arm. The small gap reduces potential wiggle in the screw. If the bar clamp slips because of wear or an oversized cut in the center pivot block, wrap a piece of sandpaper around the bar where it is seated in the slot.

Carving
in the Round

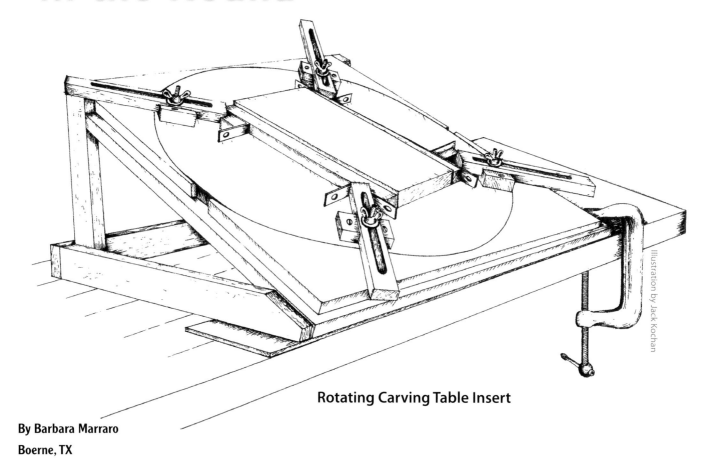

Rotating Carving Table Insert

Illustration by Jack Kochan

By Barbara Marraro
Boerne, TX

Being fairly new to relief carving, I found myself spending a lot of time turning my carvings around to achieve the most advantageous position to use my tools. This carving table, which sits on a bench, was designed to provide unlimited positioning of the relief panel.

The two main sections of the table were made from ¾"-thick medium-density fiberboard (MDF). The frame consists of ¾"-thick x 2"-wide spruce boards and a clamping board of scrap ¼"-thick plywood. The sliding brackets are ¾"-thick x 1"-wide x 8½"-long. The brackets slide in holders that measure ¾"-thick x 2¼"-wide x 1½"-deep. Other materials necessary are four ¼" x 2½" stove bolts with wing nuts and washers; four 2" corner braces; and ¾"-thick squares of hard rubber. I use the rubber

squares at the ends of the brackets to help apply pressure to the panel, especially on irregularly shaped projects. To help hold rectangular boards in place, I use 1" corner braces attached to strips of scrap wood.

The upper frame is split to allow the insert to turn freely. Even while the table is tilted at approximately 20°, I have no problem with the insert working its way out.

My table insert measures 20" in diameter. If I build another carving table, I will make it 24" and shrink the sliding bracket holders to 1" deep. As currently designed, the maximum depth of a rectangular carving that will fit on the table is about 10". These modifications will allow the table to accommodate a larger carving without making it impossible to carve in the center of the panel.

Hitch Your
Carving to a Bargain

By Richard Rayburn
Ashland, KY

I designed a tilting carver's vise from a trailer hitch ball. At a cost of around $20, it is made of components purchased at a hardware store or home center. The vise is a great substitute for expensive power arms, and it can be attached to a workbench top or a portable clamping bench.

I started with a ¾"-thick board big enough to hold the vise. I attached to it a 1½" pipe floor flange using four ⁵⁄₁₆" x 3½" carriage bolts and wing nuts. These bolts also hold an inverted pipe floor flange of the same size that keeps the trailer ball seated in the bottom flange. Although the illustration shows short bolts, I can use longer ones if I want to do some vigorous carving with mallet and chisel.

It is very important to use a lock nut on the threaded part of the trailer ball. I had to hacksaw a ¾" nut in half because there wasn't enough bolt thread left after assembly.

The steel plate to which the carving attaches measures ¼" thick x 5" x 5". It was what I had on hand. I welded a ¾" nut to the bottom of it. I later designed a plate for small carvings using a ½" pipe floor flange and welded a ¾" nut to that.

After I drilled ³⁄₁₆"-diameter holes in the top plate to use for securing my woodcarving, I screwed the plate fully onto the trailer bolt until it was tight. I then drilled a ³⁄₁₆"-diameter hole through the top plate nut and at the same time through the trailer ball bolt. This assured me the holes would line up when I inserted a ³⁄₁₆" hitch pin. The pin is necessary to prevent the plate from unscrewing.

When I carve a piece in which screw holes will be unsightly, I attach a board to the top plate and use double-stick fiberglass tape to hold the carving. Too much tape, and it will be hard to get the carving loose without damaging it.

Tilt Vise

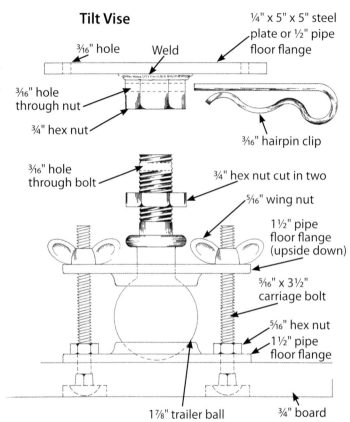

³⁄₁₆" hole   Weld   ¼" x 5" x 5" steel plate or ½" pipe floor flange

³⁄₁₆" hole through nut

¾" hex nut

³⁄₁₆" hairpin clip

³⁄₁₆" hole through bolt

¾" hex nut cut in two

⁵⁄₁₆" wing nut

1½" pipe floor flange (upside down)

⁵⁄₁₆" x 3½" carriage bolt

⁵⁄₁₆" hex nut

1½" pipe floor flange

1⅞" trailer ball   ¾" board

Materials & Tools

Materials
- 1⅞" trailer ball
- 2 each 1½" pipe floor flanges
- 2 each ¾" hex nuts
- ³⁄₁₆" hairpin clip
- 4 each ⁵⁄₁₆" x 3½" carriage bolts
- 4 each ⁵⁄₁₆" wing nuts
- 4 each ⁵⁄₁₆" hex nuts
- ¾" board
- ¼" x 5" x 5" steel plate or ½" pipe floor flange

Dust Collector:
The Bargain Version

By Elmer Jumper

Dust collectors come in all sizes and shapes and can run in the hundreds of dollars. Even the poor man's versions I read about will cost the price of a dinner at a good restaurant. But if you already have a 20" window or floor fan you can spare, my version will cost less than $10.

The secret to making the dust collector is the home air filter sold for furnaces. A pleated filter measuring 20" square x 1" thick costs as little as $4 and delivers several months' worth of performance.

Many fans have side impressions that can be knocked out. If not, drill a hole on both sides to hold eyebolts secured with nuts and fender washers. By attaching a bungee cord to the eyebolts, the filter is held in place. Make sure to check the direction of airflow recommended on the filter, and turn the fan so it acts as an exhaust unit instead of an air circulator directed at you.

The dust collector will work on the floor or on a bench top. It can even be suspended from the ceiling. Turn the knob on before hanging the fan and then plug it in to prevent a mishap.

It will effectively gather dust generated by power carving if set at a high speed. Set at a low speed, the fan will gently remove smoke created by woodburning.

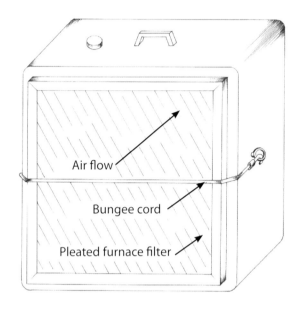

Air flow

Bungee cord

Pleated furnace filter

Dust Collection Tips

If you want to test the effectiveness of your dust collection system, an easy way to do it is to turn it on and sprinkle some talcum powder. If the dust collector takes in the talc, you know it will remove fine enough dust from the air.

An easy way to thread grounding wire through your dust collection system is to wrap the wire around a sponge. Then, go to the farthest collection point and allow the collector to suck the sponge the whole way through the system.

Garry McKinney
Martinsburg, WV

Carver's Dust Apron

One carver turned his old jogging suit into an apron that dust just slides off. Cut the legs off the pants, and then cut the legs open. He sewed the two sections of the legs together and sewed that to the jacket. He was left with a full-body dust suit with a hood. Dust wipes right off the slippery material, and his wife is happy his clothes are no longer full of dust!

Oliver Harrigan
Milwaukee, WI

A Poor Man's
Dust Collector

By Jim Smith

The fine wood dust particles created by power carving tools are a messy nuisance to say the least. At worst, they pose a real health hazard to woodcarvers. You can wear a respiration mask to protect your lungs from the floating wood particles, but for many of us, the dust is an eye irritant as well.

This project fills the need for a low-cost, efficient dust collector that can easily be assembled in a few hours with common tools. I've been using my unit for nearly two years and am very satisfied with its performance. The fan draws air and dust through the top of the unit and expels clean air through the four filters that make up the sides of the collector. Large dust particles and wood chips collect in the bottom of the box, which can easily be emptied. The advantage of this dust collector over other fan-and-filter-in-a-box units is the large surface area of the filters, which allows maximum airflow through the fan. The unit is made from items purchased at the local hardware and office supply stores. The cost is about $50. The shopping list includes the following:

Materials & Tools

Materials
- 1 circular room fan, 120 volt, 1.1 amps or similar
- ½" thick x 2' x 4' plywood
- 4 pleated furnace filters, 16" x 20"
- 2 sheets 2' x 4' foam board
- Carpenter's glue
- Packing tape
- Silicone caulking compound

Construction Details

The dust collector consists of three components: the top fan assembly, the tower or box, and the base. The efficiency and ease of construction of this dust collector depend largely on finding a suitable fan—one that has a good draw and the convenience of a power/speed selector switch mounted on the back of the casing. The fan I chose has a 12"-diameter circular fan mounted to a tilting stand. I removed the fan's protective front cover and the stand for easy attachment to the top of the box.

Although different mounting strategies for the fan can be used, I screwed and glued two support blocks to the underside of the plywood, and then screwed the fan case to these blocks. The fan has to be mounted so it draws the dust in, not blow it out.

Using a saber saw, I cut a circular opening in one of the plywood squares to accommodate the fan. To form the dust collector lid, I glued and taped four 3" x 17" foam board pieces to the sides of the plywood to form the dust collector cover.

After the glue dried, I mounted the fan to the cover. Using a silicone caulking compound, I sealed the fan to the plywood and let the caulk cure.

Cutouts

I cut the plywood and foam board pieces to the following dimensions. The foam board cut easily using a straight edge and a hobby knife. To cut the plywood, I used a table saw.

2 pieces	½" thick x 16¾" x 16¾" plywood
8 pieces	¼" thick x 3" x 17" foam board

Top Fan Assembly

• **Base:** Using glue and tape, I assembled the other plywood square and the four remaining 3" x 17" foam board pieces to create the base of the unit.

• **Filter Assembly (Tower):** I taped the four filters together to form a 20"-high rectangular tower.

• **Final Assembly:** After fitting the taped filters into the base, I placed the fan assembly and cover over the filters. My dust collector was ready for business.

A Variation

If you are "hogging away" large amounts of wood, you may wish to concentrate the airflow from a specific direction. A deflector hood can easily be constructed from foam board to fit over the top of the unit.

The Dust Collector:
A Wise Investment in Healthy Power Carving

By Louis Foshay

A dust collector is more than the luxury item some consider it to be. It is an investment in your health. The dust created from power carving or from sanding can cause health problems.

After shopping around to see what was available as well as the selling price of dust collectors, I decided it would not be difficult to make a system tailored to my needs. I designed my unit with consideration to available filter material and fans. My goal was to make it as compact as possible and to be economical regarding the filters. I also wanted a unit that could be used not only on my carving bench but also next to my scroll saw. When finished, I was able to build my model for less than $40.

The shape of the dust collector allows it to be used in an upright position or on its side. Because of the amount of suction created by the three box fans, there is no need for extended dust shields. However, they can be added with little additional cost or trouble. Friction holds the filter material in place and needs only to be pulled out and whacked against a tree or another solid object outdoors to remove most of the dust. The filter can then be replaced or, if a more thorough cleaning is desired, a shop vacuum will do the job. The filter pictured has been in use almost daily for over two years. Being retired, I carve nearly every day and it gets a workout.

The front of the dust collector with filters in place.

Here is the front with the filters removed.

Construction

Use ¾" plywood for the box. Cut the rear (R) and front (F) panels 6" x 18" long. Draw the two rectangular openings in the front panel and cut them out using a jigsaw or scroll saw. Next, arrange the fans on the rear panel so they resemble my drawing. Drill the holes for the mounting screws and countersink them if you are using flathead fasteners. Then, cut the round exit holes (H) for the exhaust air leaving the box fans using a jigsaw or scroll saw. Make the holes the diameters of the fan blades. Sand smooth both the round holes in the rear panel and the rectangular ones in the front panel.

Here is the rear of the dust collector.

The two side panels (S) need to be exactly the same size as the height of the front and rear panels—6" high x 7" long. Also, cut the top (T) and bottom (B) pieces to 7" high x 19½" long. Using glue and either brads or finishing nails 1¼" long, nail the top to the two sides panels. Secure the back flush with the three pieces just assembled with glue and nails. Scribe a line on the inside of the two sides and the top 1½" in from the front panel. The line indicates where the front panel is located, and the recess accommodates the filters. Apply glue to the bottom panel and nail in place.

Drill a hole the size of your electrical wire in the end of your box so it will be behind the front panel. If you desire, paint the box or apply a coat of polyurethane. A metal handle can be installed on the top of the box for easier handling as well as rubber feet on the bottom.

Install the box fans with the appropriate screws and wire the motors to the electrical cord that has the receptacle end removed. Cut the metal hardware cloth or rabbit wire to 6" x 18" so it fits the front opening and fasten it with small wood screws to the front panel.

When cutting the filter material, be sure to cut it a little larger than the opening. This prevents air leaks and the coarser and stiffer polyurethane will hold the other filter material as well as itself in place without fasteners. Once the filter material is installed, the unit is ready to be placed in service.

Materials & Tools

Materials
- 3 mini box fans, 115 volts, 4¾" x 4¾" x ½" deep (I used computer fans, each moves 40 cubic feet of air per minute) or 3 fans 4 ¹¹⁄₁₆" x 4 ¹¹⁄₁₆" x ½" deep that each move 65 feet of air per minute
- ¾" plywood panel at least 20" x 36"
- Heavy-duty extension cord
- 12" by 18" Varathane sanding pad (outer layer filter material)
- ¼"-thick black sponge filter material (center two layers)
- Purolator refill filter or anti-microbial treated refill (inner layer)
- 1 piece of hardware cloth or rabbit cage wire
- Switch mounted on collector or an in-line switch (optional)
- Fasteners of choice
- Wood glue of choice
- Brads or finishing nails 1¼" long
- Polyurethane finish or paint (optional)
- Metal handle and rubber feet (optional)

Tools
- Jigsaw or scroll saw
- Drill and countersink bits or bits sized for fasteners of choice
- Assorted grits of sandpaper

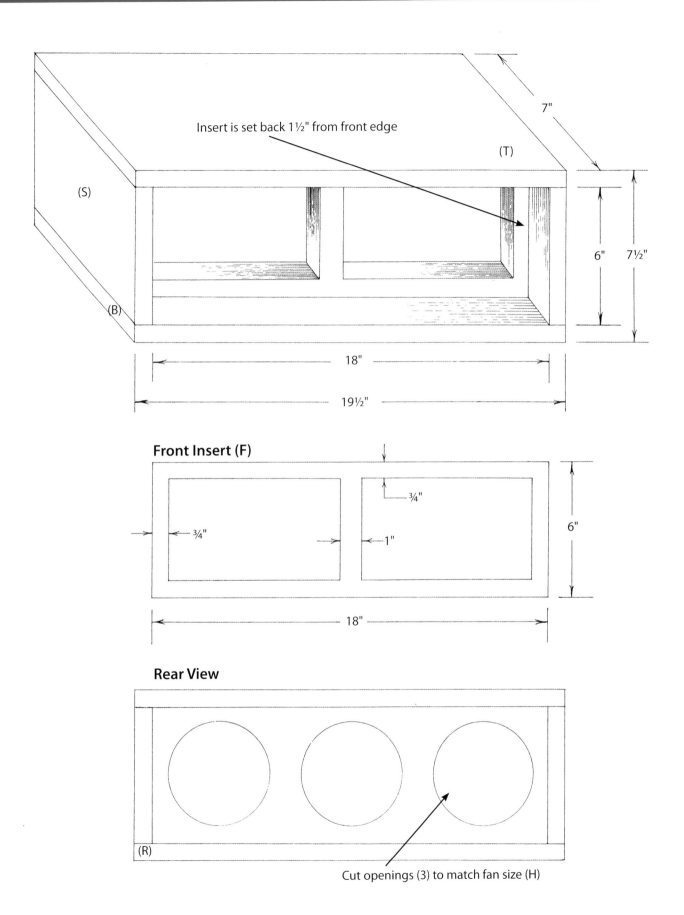

Insert is set back 1½" from front edge

(T)

(S)

(B)

7"

6"

7½"

18"

19½"

Front Insert (F)

¾"

¾"

1"

6"

18"

Rear View

(R)

Cut openings (3) to match fan size (H)

Common
Workshop Items

Ever wonder which adhesive is best for the job you're working on? This chapter covers useful information about items you're likely to have in your shop—everything you ever wanted to know about sandpaper, epoxy, and more.

Learn all about adhesives on page 52.

Adhesives Part 1: PVA and Polyurethane Glues

By Roger Schroeder

Whether I am gluing up a block of wood to sculpt a bust or laminating boards for a relief carving, I need an adhesive that is strong, reliable, and durable. While there are nearly as many glues available as there are carving tools to choose from, usually one or two are applicable for the glue-up I need to make. Let me share with you the adhesives I use for my projects and some I recently tested.

A variety of polyvinyl acetate adhesives, better known as white and yellow glues, are available at home centers, lumber retailers, and mail-order catalogs. Yellow glue in particular offers a strong bond that sands and paints easily.

Yellow and White Glues

PVA glues are the backbone of woodworking, and most woodcarvers are familiar with them. PVA stands for polyvinyl acetate. The PVAs most of us recognize are yellow and white glues, and both are as common as chips in a carving studio. They are sold in nearly every home center, craft and hobby stores, lumberyards that have a retail section, and even some supermarkets.

Although the technical data for white glue claim it bonds most porous material from paper to pottery, and it is very workable because it sets up without a lot of tackiness that can make moving the components difficult, you are better off applying yellow glue to your project. Stronger than white glue and made for both interior and exterior uses, it is the favorite of most of the woodcarvers and woodworkers I know, including myself. With a strong initial tack and fast set-up time, yellow glue makes for a easily sanded superior bond and takes paint very well. White glue tends to clog the sandpaper.

Easy Application

For a carver who is working with woods such as pine, basswood, mahogany, butternut, walnut, and other nonoily species, PVA glue is ideal. Simply spread it on surfaces to be joined—PVAs usually flow well and readily cling to wood—clamp and leave it to set up overnight. Cleanup is accomplished with water, but be careful about washing off a lot of the glue in a sink. You can end up clogging or restricting the flow in the drainpipe. It's better to rid yourself or the applicator of glue in a bucket of water or outside under a faucet.

On the Shelf

No shelf life information is provided on any PVA container I examined. I have read the typical shelf life of an opened container is anywhere from six months to a couple of years. Of course, temperature has a lot to do with how long your glue maintains its top performance. You would be wise to invest in small amounts of glue, even though it's more cost effective to purchase large containers. If the glue has been sitting around for more than a year, it just might save you heartache later on by getting rid of the container and purchasing some fresh glue.

Dark PVAs

While the assets of PVAs include easy sanding and paint application, the glue line produced is often a liability. Titebond and Elmer's have put dark glues on the market. Specifically formulated for gluing woods like walnut, cherry, and other dark species, these PVAs have a tan to light muddy color that hides the telltale glue joint while maintaining the same performance as their yellow-colored cousins. Be advised, however, that wherever excess glue, be it dark or yellow, is not sanded, scraped, or carved away, it will resist stains and show up through the finish as a blemish.

Polyurethane glues are exceptionally strong adhesives. They can, however, be irritating to the eyes, skin, and respiratory tract.

Other Pros

Since PVAs are waterbased, freezing temperatures can ruin them. Containers of the glue should be stored indoors, not in a garage in northern climates. Despite their fragility in cold weather, PVAs are not flammable, do not cause respiratory problems, and at worst they will chap the skin but will not cause burns or get absorbed into your body as a toxin. Another plus is PVAs are relatively inexpensive. A gallon of yellow glue can be purchased at your local home improvement center for about $15.

The Ultimate Adhesives

Polyurethane glues are familiar to many woodworkers. Touted by manufacturers as being extremely strong, they offer an alternative to PVAs. While you apply the adhesive as you would white or yellow glue, the similarities stop there. Unlike PVAs, polyurethane adhesives foam out and harden, resembling rising bread dough. The foam has little strength and can be pared away with almost any sharp tool. Using a carpenter's chisel to cut away the dried foam on a recent carving project, I did find some of it was exceptionally hard to remove. In fact, in a few areas chips of wood broke away as I literally pried the glue loose.

Keep the Clamps On

All of the polyurethane glue manufacturers' instructions recommend clamping time from one to five hours with a fully cured time of 24 hours. Just to be on the safe side, keep the wood clamped overnight. If you tend to be impatient to get started on the project, have something else to work on in the meantime. Because of the extreme temperature and humidity changes experienced throughout most of North America—we're not all fortunate enough to live in San Diego, California—it's best to let the wood stay clamped as long as possible so the glue sets up without the stresses of movement. What I do appreciate about the polyurethane glues is the extra working time averages about 30 minutes for the four I tested. That is considerably more time than offered by the yellow glues I put to use on a regular basis.

Each of the four glues I worked with is labeled waterproof. By waterproof, I assume the bond will not hold if the wood is submersed for a long period. One of the container labels indicates the glue is not recommended for structural applications below a waterline. The real test of these products is to laminate a sign panel and mount it outdoors for an indefinite period. The results should prove interesting.

The high-relief basswood eagle was laminated with Gorilla Glue, a polyurethane adhesive that claims to be "The Toughest Glue on Planet Earth."

Polyurethane glues foam out as they dry. The foam, which has little strength, can be removed with almost any sharp tool.

Polyurethane Cautions

These glues do have liabilities that include skin rashes, respiratory problems, even dizziness. As I am writing this feature with four containers of the adhesive in front of me, each carefully sealed, I find my eyes starting to burn and my throat getting sore. I know for certain that it is not the computer that is the irritant.

Handling the glue with gloves is mandatory. I strongly recommend wearing disposable latex gloves when using polyurethane glues. When I accidentally touched the still uncured glue of a sample I was testing, it left a stain on my finger that took several days to disappear.

Also be advised these glues have limited shelf life. Titebond's polyurethane glue has a life of only one year

if left unopened and stored where the temperature is below 80°. Gorilla Glue has three times the unopened shelf life and up to one year if the container is used. Neither Probond nor Excel One offers information on shelf life. To be on the safe side, I would make sure all polyurethane glues are used up within a year's time. If not, then disposal is in order. To keep track of shelf life, put the date of purchase on a piece of masking tape and attach it to the container.

Keeping the Joints Tight

Despite the strength of these two chemically different adhesives, the haunting liability of both PVA and polyurethane glues is they do not fill gaps. When boards or even small components of a carving are joined, surfaces must be touching with almost mathematical precision. When they are not, the holding power of the glue is negligible. If filling gaps and durability are your goals, then read about epoxies on page 56.

What's New

Glue run-out from clamping pressure is the bane of woodcarvers and woodworkers. The glue dries in the most inappropriate places, including on the clamps. Elmer's has come out with Carpenter's Wood Glue Paste. Gel-like in its consistency, the product still has squeeze-out, but it does not run. This may take some getting used to because application is accomplished with a putty knife, stiff brush, or for very large surfaces, a trowel. Yellow in color, Carpenter's Wood Glue Paste still offers great bonding strength, and it's sandable and paintable.

Another PVA glue, one I have yet to try, has been developed by Titebond. Offering an extended formula, the manufacturer claims the new product has triple the open time of the original adhesive with the same clamping duration and bonding strength. In actual working time, this translates to about 15 minutes at a moderate temperature and humidity level. Both a general-purpose and a waterproof glue are now on the market.

Editor's note: The glues described by no means make up a complete list. New products appear on the market regularly. Check your favorite catalog or home improvement center for the latest entries into the field of adhesives. Be sure to read product descriptions and instructions thoroughly.

Most glues have a limited shelf life, so it's advisable to write the date of purchase on the container.

An old trick for testing how good the glue joints of laminated boards are is to cut a thin cross section of the panel and break it. If the wood splits along the joint, the boards will likely separate in the future.

Adhesives Part 2:
Epoxies

By Roger Schroeder

Epoxies have a key role in my workshop. If I am looking for a strong bond to make a knife that includes a wooden handle joined to a steel blade, I turn to epoxy. If it's an outdoor sign requiring boards being joined, I again look on my shelf for an epoxy adhesive. And if it's a project that needs pieces of wood bonded that don't have perfectly mated surfaces, I reach for an epoxy product.

What makes epoxies different from PVA and polyurethane glues is they come in two containers, two tubes, or in two chambers of a syringe-like mixer. For epoxies to harden and then cure, a resin and a hardener must chemically interact with each other. How long that takes depends upon the product, but the range is from several hours to overnight.

Dispensing Epoxy

Epoxies have been around for half a century, and they have touched our lives in many ways, from crafting projects to making repairs. Few adults I've met have not used, or at least seen, for example, the epoxy dispenser that automatically squeezes out equal parts of the resin and hardener. For woodcarvers, the dispensers are typically called five-minute or quick-setting products. I once thought they had replaced the squeezable tube products, but tubes with quick-to-harden epoxies are still readily available. Mix the resin and hardener together, smear it on the wood, clamp the pieces together, and a strong bond exists in minutes. While believing we can have a cured glue joint in the time it takes to drink a cup of coffee on the run is a pleasant thought, those advertised attributes are very misleading. As described

Epoxies are especially useful when bonding wood and metal, as seen here in knifemaking.

Sign carvers like Greg Krockta take advantage of waterproof epoxies that offer great strength for longer-lasting signs.

in the directions of one fast-drying product, mixing of the resin and hardener and the assembly of parts must be immediate. Set-up time is five minutes, a process you can judge when a stirring tool such as a toothpick is left in the mix. When you can't remove it, and that usually occurs before that coffee cup is drained, setting time has elapsed. However, before the joinery can be handled and used, expect several hours to go by. One product I examined claims full strength is not attained until 24 hours have passed. And even that number is subject to increase depending on the temperature. A cool shop will slow down the cure and a warm one will speed it up. One product, however, offers a temperature range of minus 65° to 225° Fahrenheit. While it's unlikely you will be bonding wood in the Antarctic or in an oven, your best bet is to use these epoxies at a room temperature of approximately 70°. Working with them in an unheated garage in the winter may not give you the cure you are seeking. And be advised some epoxies will freeze.

Mixing equal amounts of epoxies that come in tubes or containers means utilizing an old spoon or a container with measuring increments. Either method tends to be imprecise, yet I have not had problems if the amounts were not exact.

Stirring is essential, no matter what epoxy you use. One container product I tested, G-1, required mixing equal parts of resin and hardener for five minutes. After that, I had to let it stand for 20 minutes. However, the working time is an hour if the directions are followed.

Two Tones

Whether you have a syringe, tubes, or containers, you will notice the resin and hardener have slightly different colors—one clear, one amber. The advantages are threefold. First, you can visually check that equal amounts are being dispensed. Second, you will not make the mistake of mixing two equal amounts of the same part. And third, the likelihood of contaminating one part with the other is lessened. The first time I used a two-container epoxy, I poked my stirrer-toothpick into both. The next time I went to use the epoxy, the resin container was hard enough to hammer nails.

Two-part West System, a marine epoxy, is dispensed with pumps that pre-measure the amounts of resin and hardener required.

Making the Grade

Two grades of epoxies are available—consumer and commercial. While consumer-grade epoxy is typically found in hardware and home centers, you will likely have to go to a woodworker's catalog for the commercial grade. The advantages of the latter include greater strength and longevity. A typical commercial product is T-88, described as a structural epoxy adhesive. According to the specifications, it is waterproof, will cure in any thickness without shrinking, and it is unaffected by most chemicals. T-88 will harden in six to nine hours at 77°, and reach full strength in 24 hours. If used in temperatures near freezing, expect a week before full cure is reached.

I have used T-88 with success. Working time is about 30 minutes, more than enough for most projects. When dry, it is non-brittle, and it can be carved and sanded. And like the consumer epoxies, it comes in two colors—clear and amber. What I particularly like about T-88 is both the resin and hardener must be squeezed out through narrow spouts. The design greatly reduces the risk of contaminating one part with the other.

Pumping Epoxy

Familiar to woodworkers in the signmaking and boatbuilding industry is West System. Described by many as a state-of-the-art commercial adhesive especially formulated for outdoor conditions and materials such as fiberglass, the two parts are dispensed with calibrated pumps. These pumps, which are purchased separately, push out five parts of resin for one part of hardener.

Attempting to mix by weight or volume is asking for trouble, so the pumps are crucial to getting the right mix. The pumps are labeled with a color that matches the printing on the containers. While it's fine to keep the pumps attached to the containers, check that there is no leakage.

While West System has superior properties for bonding and repairs, it does come with some caveats. As the epoxy cures, it generates heat. Use a shallow mixing container to prevent heat buildup. It's enough to melt plastic, and it will burn.

For best results that allow you a working time of 20 to 25 minutes, use West System in a room where the temperature is about 70°. At that temperature, curing to a solid state should be between 9 and 12 hours.

What to Avoid

Many of these epoxies cause skin sensitization, especially after repeated contact. Irritations and rashes may appear after a while, and they will continue to plague you with use. I strongly recommend wearing rubber or latex gloves when mixing epoxies. Having a hypersensitivity to chemicals, I have found that after only a few chance contacts with the chemicals, I started to develop itchiness. Scrubbing with soap and water is mandatory when epoxies come in contact with your skin.

The two parts of an epoxy are vigorously mixed together. Wearing disposable or latex gloves should be mandatory when working with epoxy.

Gap Filler

Unlike the PVA and polyurethane adhesives, epoxies have wonderful gap-filling capabilities. Cracks can be filled and joints don't have to be matched with precision. The best filler is one mixed with wood dust. Talking with other woodcarvers, I've come to the conclusion that a mix of one part dust to three parts epoxy is the right proportion. Too much dust thins out the adhesive and reduces the bond. Too little wood and the epoxy, which dries clear, will not disguise the gap or crack.

Epoxy to the Rescue

Some woods, because of their oily natures, present problems when gluing. I've found this to be true with species like teak and rosewood. The resins in these woods tend to repel water, so adhesives like PVA and polyurethane don't get absorbed into the grain. Many technical sources recommend wiping the surfaces to be joined with lacquer thinner or denatured alcohol, but resins will still interfere with the bond. Epoxy comes to the rescue because it does not need to have the oily surfaces neutralized.

Clamping

PVA and polyurethane glues must be clamped with considerable pressure. These adhesives have negligible gap-filling strength, so tightly mated surfaces are necessary. Epoxy, however, requires minimal pressure. In fact, overclamping will cause a starved joint, a problem that will result in the bond failing.

While holding a laminated sign together until the epoxy cures must be done with clamps, there are many creative ways to bond small pieces of wood without applying too much pressure. Tape is one solution for small projects, but it can leave a sticky residue. Rubber bands are another possibility. The advantage of the rubber band is you can exert as much or as little pressure as you need. Use a small stick and make a tourniquet to tighten the band if necessary. Then, tape the stick in place. If that doesn't work, try a Quick-Grip micro bar clamp. Available at home centers, these clamps have jaw openings as small as 4¼".

Clean Up

Runs and drips are not a problem when bonding wood or filling gaps. I let the epoxy cure and remove the excess with a knife or other carving tool. Epoxies can also be filed and sanded—rotary bits may clog—so I don't fret much about the adhesive drying where it is not wanted. However, if it should drip on one of my expensive laminated maple bench tops, I do want to remove it before it dries.

Packaging and container instructions sometimes recommend clean up with soap and water. I find denatured alcohol a better choice. Although it is a hazardous liquid, it removes epoxy with miraculous speed, and it evaporates almost instantly, leaving no chemical residue. Lacquer thinner and acetone will also remove yet-to-harden epoxy. If you want to avoid harsh and dangerous chemicals, try white vinegar followed by a water wash.

A Good Investment

While a product like West System can run $70 or more, most epoxies are relatively inexpensive, although the quantity is small compared to containers of PVA and polyurethane glues. I purchased Devcon 5 Minute Fast Drying Epoxy—in two ½-oz. tubes—for $3.99 plus tax at a local hardware store. For carvers who want to bond unlike materials, such as wood and metal, epoxies are the best adhesives to use. They are also an excellent choice for oily hardwoods. What may be the best argument for investing in epoxies is their shelf life. Most PVA and polyurethane glues need to be replaced after a year or so. Epoxies can last for years without degradation.

Epoxy Put to the Test

I designed a running man with one leg extended out behind his body. With grain running perpendicular to the leg, I knew I was facing the risk of breakage. It was time to put epoxy to the test.

After cutting out the figure, I removed the leg at the knee. I then cut a replacement section from the knee to the foot, with the grain running parallel to it, and joined it to the body. I used a small, slightly undersized dowel to aid the joint. It provided more surface for the epoxy. Second, it prevented the leg from shifting when I clamped it.

The design for the running man predicts that the outstretched leg will be a weak point of the carving, subject to breakage if it should fall or if there is a defect in the grain as it is carved.

The leg is removed at the knee joint with a fine-toothed saw. A replacement leg will have the grain running through the length of the leg, not perpendicular to it.

A file is used to smooth the areas to be joined.

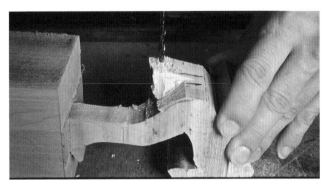
A hole is drilled in the body to accommodate the dowel.

Crash Test

After waiting several hours for the epoxy to dry—I used a slow-setting product—I was able to lift the cutout by the leg. The glue joint held. Next, I decided to put the cutout to a crash test. I put the carving on the edge of my workbench, leg aimed for the wooden floor of my shop, and let if fall. My workbench top is 36" from the floor. I next dropped it from six feet. The leg remained intact with no visible damage.

Editor's Note: When using an epoxy adhesive, wear latex or rubber gloves and make sure there is adequate ventilation. If you are sensitive to chemical fumes, make sure you wear a respirator. Acetone, denatured alcohol, or mineral spirits will work as a solvent to remove unwanted epoxy before it has dried.

The new leg is ready to be joined to the body.

A crash test is held with the carving being dropped onto the replacement leg from a height of 36". The leg survives the fall with no visible damage.

Glue Chart

Brand	Working Time	Cure Time	Waterproof	Cleanup/ Solvent	Irritant	Safety Equipment	Strength
Elmer's Glue-All (white)	35 min.	overnight	no	water	no	none	fair
PVA Elmer's Carpenter's Wood Glue (interior)	30 min.	overnight	no	water	no	none	excellent
Elmer's Carpenter's Wood Glue (exterior)	30 min.	overnight	yes	water	no	none	excellent
Titebond	10–30 min.	overnight	no	water	no	none	excellent
Titebond II	60 min.	overnight	yes	water	no	none	excellent
Excel One	0–30 min.	12 hrs.	yes	acetone	eyes, skin	latex or rubber	excellent
Polyurethane Gorilla Glue	1–4 hours	24 hrs.	yes	denatured alcohol	eyes, skin	latex or rubber	excellent
Probond	15 min.	24 hrs.	yes	mineral spirits	eyes, skin	latex or rubber	excellent
Titebond	30 min.	4 hrs.	yes	mineral spirits	eyes, skin	latex or rubber	excellent

Epoxy Chart

Brand	Working Time	Cure Time	Waterproof	Irritant	Strength
Devcon	5 min.	1 hr.	no	eyes, skin, respiratory system	excellent
Industrial Formulators 5 Cure	5 min.	10 min.	yes	eyes and skin	good
Industrial Formulators G-1	60 min.	24 hr.	yes	eyes and skin	excellent
Loctite	5 min.	24 hr.	yes	eyes, skin, respiratory system	good
Super Glue	30 min.	24 hr.	no	eyes and skin	good
System Three T-88	30–40 min.	24 hr.	yes	eyes, skin, respiratory system	excellent
West System using 105 Resin, 206 Hardener	20–25 min.	9–12 hr.	yes	eyes, skin, respiratory system	excellent

All About
Sandpaper

By Mike Way, contributed to
and photographed by Roger Schroeder

Many carvers, especially those doing caricatures or chip carvings, may frown at the mention of sandpaper, but I tackle projects from ornamental pieces to wildfowl that benefit greatly from some judiciously applied hand sanding. In fact, I consider sanding to be one of the most important steps in determining the final appearance of my carvings.

Why Sandpaper?

Even in the age of the pyramids, craftsmen used sand to shape and polish their projects. Centuries later, woodworkers glued sand or ground glass—the English sometimes refer to sandpaper as glass paper—to a backing. Or, they used sharkskin where available because of its abrasive texture. Today, minerals are still applied to a backing, including synthetics that have been around for a long time, such as aluminum oxide and silicon carbide. Of note to woodcarvers are the newly engineered minerals that have been designed for optimum performance for specific applications.

Whatever the material used, the goal is the same: to cut wood and ultimately smooth it. But unlike an edge tool or a rotary bit, sandpaper cuts only on a minute scale, so patience is a must. Realize, too, that as minerals break down or become dull, they cannot be sharpened. Consequently, sandpaper, while very useful, ultimately becomes the most disposable tool in your shop.

The array of sanding materials and accessories on the market often makes choosing the right product mind boggling.

Gritty Issues

Find a piece of very coarse sandpaper—60 grit, for example—and take a close look at it. You will see what looks like hard, jagged-edged, grain-size bits of minerals. The actual determination for grit is a screening process that separates the minerals by size. The screen for 60 grit will have 60 wires per inch in both the warp and the weft or 360 holes per square inch. This allows for quite a bit of undersized material and invariably, due to the process, some oversized. The Europeans, on the other hand, use a much more refined screening process that results in a very uniform mineral size. All papers made using the European process have the letter P in the rating. The Europeans also use a slightly different wire size in the fine screens that produces a slightly coarser material than our grit ratings. This explains why they seem to cut faster. 3M is now using the European process for their better papers.

Turn to the back of a sheet of sandpaper for a wealth of information. This paper is aluminum oxide, 100 grit, open coat.

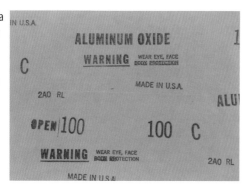

How much wood you can remove depends on grit size. Turn a sheet of sandpaper over, and you will find a lot of printed information including the brand, the kind of abrasive mineral used, and a grit number. The lower the number, the rougher the sandpaper; the higher the number, the finer the paper. It's easy to see individual particles of very coarse sandpaper, such as 60 grit, but when looking at a piece of 600-grit paper, you won't see much more than a relatively smooth surface unless it is viewed under a strong magnifying glass.

Another factor that enters into an understanding of sandpaper is the bond. Sandpapers are either open or closed coat. Coat refers to how densely the abrasive grit adheres to the surface. Open coat has greater spacing between the grains, which prevents it from clogging up as quickly with wood residue. Closed coat means 100% of the surface is covered with grit. The paper has good finishing properties, but will clog more rapidly with sanded material.

Here are ranges of grit size and their degree of coarseness and fineness:

> 40 to 60 = coarse
>
> 80 to 100 = medium coarse
>
> 120 to 180 = medium
>
> 220 to 320 = fine
>
> 360 and up = very fine

Try sanding a carving or even a rough board, working through several grits in order of increasing number. Then, rub your fingers over the wood after each sanding. You will be amazed at how much change in the surface can be detected with just the fingertips. If that isn't convincing enough, hold a strong light at a fairly oblique angle to the surface after each grit has done its job. Light and shadow will easily reveal your progress.

15 Tips for Using Sandpaper

1. Regain your focus. Sanding helps you determine where to remove additional wood throughout the carving process. Whenever I lose the focus of what I want the final piece to look like, I put down the tools and spend some time sanding. The shape of duck heads often confuses me, and I have to stop carving to visualize exactly where and how much wood needs to be removed. When I reach a spot like this, I put down the cutting tools and sand everything smooth while contemplating what needs to come off next. Regardless of the piece being carved, this change in focus allows my hands, eyes, and mind some quality time to perfect a shape that is not only pleasing to the eye but also to the touch.

One gauge I use to judge the quality of my carvings is the willingness of people to touch or handle the finished pieces. Time spent sanding helps me achieve the final shapes necessary to achieve this. However, used indiscriminately, sandpaper can blur small forms and take the sharpness away from where it needs to be retained. Making a shape smooth does not automatically make the shape a good one.

2. Don't skip the scratches. Start with a coarse-grit paper and progress through a series of finer grits until the desired finish is achieved. The reason is that each finer piece of sandpaper removes scratches left by the previous grit. If you think skipping grits will save time, you may end up sanding longer just to remove scratches left from the previous sanding.

3. Sanding across the grain is no gain. I'm sure you've heard an old adage that warns about sanding across the grain. Taking that approach produces deep scratches too hideous to look at and challenging to remove. But, most carvers don't realize more wood is removed when you sand across the grain. A compromise for early stages of sanding is to sand at a moderate angle to the grain. More material is abraded away, but the scratches are less visible. However, as you work incrementally through the finer grits of sandpaper, sand only with the grain.

4. Save the cutting edge. Because sandpaper sheds its particles, make sure you remove them with a cloth or old brush before carving. Grit quickly dulls a finely honed cutting edge.

Heavy coats of primer and paint, as seen in this photo, will fill scratches left by coarse sandpaper that may be otherwise impossible to hide.

5. Prime for smoothness. If you are painting a project, consider applying a heavy coat of primer, which fills small scratches left by coarser paper. Then, smooth the primer with a medium-grit paper and finish up with fine grit.

6. Beware of oversanding. Consider the kind of wood you are carving before oversanding. Soft and coarse-grained woods, such as cedar, do not need as much fine sanding as basswood, which does not require the same effort as a harder wood like oak. In general, softwoods take less work to sand smooth than hardwoods, and you can probably skip some grits in your incremental sanding.

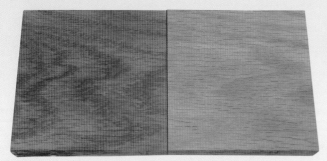

How a stain soaks into the wood after sanding is sometimes dramatic. The oak block on the left was sanded with 100-grit paper, the block on the right with a series of papers ending with 220 grit. Both were given the same stain.

7. The stain game. When sanding, keep in mind that oversanding to the point of polishing the wood surface limits the amount of stain the wood can absorb. And if a stain is used, the primary goal is to sand out nicks or scratches that will otherwise be magnified when the stain dries. If the imperfections are bothersome, you will probably have to re-sand.

8. Fresh sandpaper, please. Use fresh sandpaper whenever possible. Remember, the primary advantages of this tool are it is fairly inexpensive and disposable.

9. A question of balance. When using water as a lubricant, do not let the surface dry out. When excessive wet waste builds up, wash it away.

10. Upon further review. If the paper becomes clogged after only a short period of use, check the surface being sanded. If damp, let it dry out thoroughly. If it is too resinous, try a different type of paper.

A sanding block, which helps ride over soft spots in the wood, can be as simple as a pointed dowel wrapped with sandpaper.

11. Sand evenly. Simply holding sandpaper in your fingers can result in uneven sanding. The paper sinks into the softer areas and rides high over the harder ones, resulting in hills and valleys. Use sanding blocks or sticks whenever possible because they ride over the harder areas and prevent the softer ones from forming depressions. These devices also allow you to apply both hands to the sanding process, and greater force can be exerted. Blocks and sticks can be made from furring strips, dowels, pieces of molding, or paint stirrers. These can be quickly and easily shaped for almost any project. Simply wrap or glue the sandpaper around the block. If you desire a lighter touch with the sandpaper, cut out a pad from a piece of sheet cork and glue it to the block. Even a piece of packing Styrofoam can be shaped and covered with sandpaper.

12. Keep it unclogged. Whenever possible, remove glue from the surface prior to sanding. Glue tends to quickly clog sandpaper. Use a knife, chisel, or sharpened scraper if necessary.

13. Repair with moisture. To repair a dent in the wood, place a small drop of hot water on the damaged area. Similarly, if a super-smooth finish is desired, wipe the surface with a warm, damp cloth. The warm water will penetrate the surface and raise the grain, which can then be sanded smooth. In some woods, the stain or sealer will raise the grain, requiring additional light sanding.

14. Try scraping. For an extra-fine polished look, scrape the surface as the final step before applying a finish. Again, raise the grain with a damp cloth; then, use the sharp edge of a piece of steel, glass, or plastic held perpendicular to the surface and scrape with light pressure in the direction of the grain. Professional cabinetmaker's scrapers made from steel can be purchased in most fine woodworking catalogs along with directions for their use.

15. Keep paper cool and dry. Store sandpaper in a cool, dry place and keep the sheets flat. If they were purchased in a cardboard sleeve or box, leave them in the packaging. With the exception of wet-and-dry paper, dampness may cause the adhesive to fail or weaken, and grains will detach.

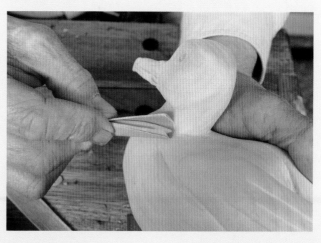

The Paper Chase

Walk into the local home improvement center or hardware store, and you'll discover an array of sandpaper. Many brands come in packs, some with as many as 50 sheets. Here's an overview of the four most common sandpapers and their properties:

Emery paper is cloth backed with water-soluble glue. A natural, black abrasive, emery is ideal for polishing and smoothing metal and typically requires an oil lubricant. The backing is a denim material and very durable. While it is commonly found with other sandpapers, it is not recommended for wood because it does not sand wood well and clogs quickly.

Silicon carbide is a very sharp and very hard mineral used in wet/dry sandpapers. An interesting aspect of silicon carbide is that as it dulls, friction causes the dull material to cleave, or fracture off, leaving a new sharp surface. Because the backing and glue are designed for use with water, the paper can be rinsed to remove any clogging. Some silicon carbide papers are treated with a zinc stearate coating to prevent clogging. This gray soap-like coating sometimes leaves a residue that can reduce the adherence and finish of water-based finishes, although it does not affect oil-based finishes. Because it sheds grit, silicon carbide should be used only for final sanding or sanding between finishes to avoid dulling your tools. I used to rely on silicon carbide paper a great deal since it came in a wider range of grits and lasted longer because of its heavier weight backing. New materials, which are described below, have eclipsed my usage of silicon carbide almost completely.

Garnet is another mineral used for sandpaper and is well suited for wood. Sharp, yet not terribly hard, garnet will actually dull quicker when used on paints and varnishes than when used on wood because it requires greater heat and friction to fracture the surface. Garnet especially shines when used on end grains, although it can actually burnish the surface, which will affect how stains and colors are absorbed. It dulls as it sheds particles, so care should be given to dust off the carving to protect your finely honed tools.

Aluminum oxide is a good all-around paper for woodworking. It is both cheap and readily available and does not fracture, as do the silicon carbide and garnet. I use coarse-grit aluminum oxide primarily for rough work because it removes wood quickly. For example, I follow up with the sandpaper after using a rasp to rough out decoy heads and bodies. I work with the finer grades between finish coats or whenever a cheap, disposable paper is all that is required.

Some of the specialty sanding products use a "semi-friable" **ceramic aluminum oxide**, designed to re-fracture to increase the life of the paper. If you are not sure what type of mineral is on the paper, it might be a good idea to dust off the piece carefully after sanding.

Backing Materials

There seems to be a rule of thumb that the stiffer the backing of your sandpaper sheet, the deeper and faster the cuts made will be. Softer backings provide a smoother finish. Here are three backings you should know:

Ordinary paper is a cheap backing, although it seems to be adequate for most sandpaper. Paper-backed sandpaper for power tools usually has more durability than paper sold for hand sanding. Don't expect this material to last long, especially when used vigorously. It creases and ultimately tears.

Waterproof paper is essential when the sandpaper is used with a lubricant, such as water. Turn over a piece of this paper, described above as wet/dry, and you will notice the back has a darker, glossier appearance than its ordinary paper counterpart.

Cloth-backed sandpaper is the most durable of the three and should not be confused with emery cloth. Bird carvers, in particular, favor this paper because of its flexibility. I find it extremely helpful for getting into small areas and for its flexibility on curved surfaces. I also like it for final shaping of bird bills and feathers. Although expensive, a little goes a long way, and it lasts long time.

True Grit

Before reading this, you probably thought sanding was a basic process, and it is—once you get a feel for grit and types of paper available. For all occasions, then, I keep lots of sandpaper on hand in almost every grit from 60 to 400. I have been so pleased with the European papers and SandBlaster products that I have stopped stocking the silicon carbide products.

Sanding Products Worth a Closer Look

Newer to the market are 3M's SandBlaster and Norton's 3X products. Available as papers, pads, and sponges, these accessories use specially engineered particles with anti-load coatings that do not contain zinc stearate and will not affect finishes. A real advantage of the blocks and pads, which are flexible and tear resistant, is they can be washed and reused numerous times. More expensive than other brands, these durable products cut faster and last longer, making them well worth the added expense. Check out your local home improvement center or hardware store for availability.

Swiss and German-made cloth-backed sandpapers are real friends to woodcarvers. Backed with denim-weight cloth, they have abrasive grits made from sharp, extra-tough materials. These sandpapers come in rolls, ranging in grit size from 80 to 500. Durable, they can be flexed and rolled to fit sanding devices or folded to get into crevices. Power carvers favor cloth-backed papers because they can be wrapped around a split mandrel or a foam-cushioned sanding drum.

The nail files come with foam and aluminum centers. They are also available as mini-nail files. All are excellent for sanding a variety of contours.

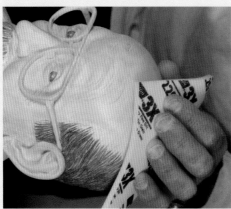

Newer products on the market, such as Norton's 3X sanding pads, are flexible, tear resistant and outlast most papers.

Shop-Made Sanding Bow

I made this sanding bow from imitation wood lattice. Home improvement stores sell the ¼" thick x 1¼" wide plastic material, which is a dream to bend. The sanding bow works great to smooth surfaces without changing the overall shape of the piece.

Rip the plastic material down to approximately 1 1/16" wide. Dunk the plastic in about 3" of boiling water. Make sure the area you want to bend is submerged in the water. After the plastic is hot, grip it carefully and bend it to shape. I found that an outside angle of about 75° works best. Hold the material under cold water to lock the plastic at the desired angle.

Cut the handgrip from scrap wood. I cut the wood to 1 1/16" x 1 1/8" x 6". Cut off the ends at a 70° angle. Glue the handgrip in the center of the straight section of the plastic. Round the edges of the handgrip.

Create clamps to hold the sandpaper strips in place. Cut four pieces of the lattice material to 1 1/16" x 1 1/16". Drill a ¼"-diameter hole through all four pieces. Drill matching holes through the ends of the bow. Attach two #10-32 x 5/16" long tee nuts to two of the square lattice pieces. Glue these scraps to the inside of the bow. Round one end of the other two lattice pieces. Use two #10-32 x 1" long machine screws to attach the rounded lattice pieces to the outside of the bow.

I use Klingspor gold sanding strips in the bow. Control the tension with the length of the sanding strip. The shorter you make the strip, the higher the tension will be. Cut the strip 1" longer than you want the belt to be. Fold the final ½" on both ends back upon itself. This fold helps the lattice clamps hold the belt in place. Tighten the machine screws and lattice clamps down on the sanding strip to lock the strip in place.

Eric A. Seiffer
North Chili, NY

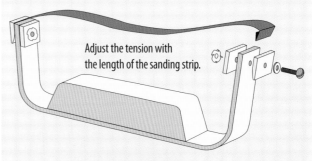

Adjust the tension with the length of the sanding strip.

A shop-made sanding tool is ideal for smoothing curved surfaces.

Shop-Made
Holding Devices

By Roger Schroeder

Carvers tend to be innovative—and with the odd shapes carvings can take on, many commercial holding devices just won't work. That is why carvers design, or adapt, their own holding devices. The variety of designs is endless, but most can be broken down into a few simple approaches. All of them can be made with commonly available materials.

Hand Vise

Many wildfowl carvers use a painting stick because the bird is too small to hold. A painting stick is a length of square lumber or a section of a large-diameter dowel with a screw imbedded in one end with the point sticking out. Pre-drill a hole in the bottom of the bird, screw the dowel into the bird, and you have an instant holding device.

Carver's Frame

Early carvers used a simple screw to hold a carving to a bench. This carver's screw comes up through a hole in the work surface and locks the carving in place with the aid of a handle. One way to make one is with a large lag screw and washer. Two carver's screws combine to make a holding fixture Europeans call a carver's frame.

John and Nancy Burke, of Ithaca, Neb., designed and built an American-style carver's frame that accomplishes what expensive vises do and then some. It allows a carving to be rotated horizontally and vertically, and it also allows you to adjust the height of the project.

A carver's frame allows the carving to be rotated both horizontally and vertically.

Using a length of 4" x 6" lumber for the post and a piece of 3" thick x 12" x 20" board for the clamping platform, the Burkes' carver's frame is stable without tying up an entire workbench. The post is supported by a set of steel legs, put together sawhorse-style, and a crossbar. One bench screw allows the platform to be rotated, the other screw holds the carving, which can then be turned a full 360° to the platform.

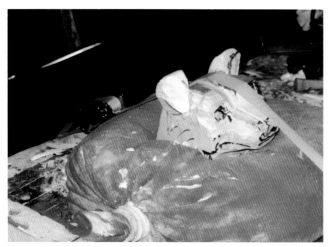

Russ Robinson's sandbag and web clamp make for a sturdy, but flexible, holding fixture.

Carver's Sandbag

A simple sandbag is useful to hold carvings with fragile areas that need support and can't be held by screws, clamps, or vises. Sandbags also work well to hold a large carving that has to be turned so often that clamps prove impractical. Fill a plastic trash can liner with strained beach sand, and put that into an old canvas sports bag.

Russ Robinson of Grand Rapids, Mich., snugs a carving down onto a canvas-covered sandbag and provides more support with a web clamp wrapped around the carving, sandbag, and workbench.

A rope clamp is a cost-saving device that puts a strong hold on a carving.

The Rope Clamp

A rope wrapped around your carving and threaded through a hole in your workbench is a great way to hold an irregularly-shaped carving.

To turn the rope into a holding device, make sure it is long enough to go around the project and pass through a hole in the bench. Then tie it off just far enough above the floor to comfortably put a foot into the loop.

Paper and Glue

A traditional method of making a temporary joint is to use newspaper and wood glue. When working with small relief pieces, such as appliqués, even the most compact clamp will get in the way of the carving tools.

Newspaper is just the right thickness for this clamping method. Thicker paper contributes to a weaker bond. Make sure the back of your carving is flat, then apply wood glue to a piece of scrap plywood or some other warp-free board and the back of your carving. Clamp the project and backing board together with a layer of newspaper between them, and let the glue dry overnight.

Carpet Tape

Another temporary way to bond a carving to its backing plate is with double-sided carpet tape.

Carver's Bench Hook

Carvers, such as Joel Hull, have adapted a traditional woodworker's bench hook to hold irregularly shaped carvings.

The bench hook is a board that hooks itself to the edge of the workbench, thanks to a cleat nailed or screwed to the underside. Another cleat is attached to the top to act as a stop. Once the hook is in place, the woodworker can use it for sawing, chisel work, and hand plane work.

The carver's version of the bench hook has large holes, into which a cam is inserted. Attached to a dowel sized to fit the holes on the board, the cam is positioned near the carving. The side of the cam bulges out so that when it rotates, it locks the carving against the stop, another cam, or a dowel. The cam is turned in the opposite direction to unlock the carving.

Tools

No matter what type of carving you prefer, you'll use tools to remove wood. These essential tools—knives, V-tools, mallets, files, drawknives, and more—are covered in detail here. Learn about the selection of mallets available; how to make a depth guide for relief carving; or even how to make your own miniature carving tools.

Mallets, disposable carving knives, and traditional carving tools are just a few of the tools discussed in this chapter.

The Traditional
European-Style Carving Knife

By Andy Fairchok

The design of the traditional European-style carving knife is the result of more than 300 years of evolution. The handle shape is moderately slim, delicately curved, and long enough that it can easily be gripped in the fingers. The long, slim handle lends itself to everything you expect from a knife, including good reach, leverage, and the so-called pencil grip. Holding the knife as you would hold a pencil affords absolute control for very fine detail work.

The cutting edge is in line with the center axis of the handle. This gives you considerably more control since the fingers can easily make minute changes.

A carving knife is best held at the base of the fingers where they join the palm of the hand. The depth of cut is more easily controlled, as is the slicing motion. Holding a knife in the fist requires greater movement of the wrist and arm, limiting control and making carving difficult.

Push the knife. When pushing the knife away from yourself, back up the blade with the thumb of the non-gripping hand. Start the cut at the back of the blade and slide the cutting edge toward its point.

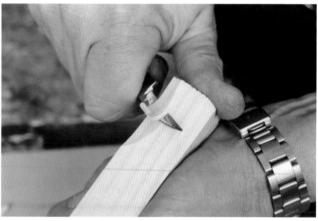

Make a draw cut. A slicing action is done when pulling the blade toward yourself in a draw cut. The thumb of the non-gripping hand is securely braced on a safe area of the wood for control.

Finger Savers

I wear rubber finger tips as a thumb guard. They usually cost about $1.99 a dozen at office supply stores. Be sure to choose one large enough to fit your thumb. When it wears out, replace it.

Linda Taylor
Midland, MI

Use the pencil grip. The traditional European knife can be gripped as you would hold a pencil. Because of its slim profile, the knife is easy to control in this position.

Custom-Made
Detail Knife

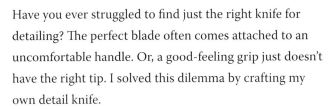

By Lynn Diel

Have you ever struggled to find just the right knife for detailing? The perfect blade often comes attached to an uncomfortable handle. Or, a good-feeling grip just doesn't have the right tip. I solved this dilemma by crafting my own detail knife.

My detail knife takes the components of a hobby knife and fits them into a custom-made handle. Economical in cost, the repackaged knife gives me better control and the ability to rotate the blade in the direction that will make the best cut. After using it, I can loosen the blade and reverse it so the sharp end is inside the knife. Both the cutting edge and my hands are safe from harm. I have made over a dozen of these knives for members of a local carving club, and all the recipients appreciate having one.

Construction

Make sure you have a hobby knife that disassembles. I recommend an X-Acto Gripster Knife with a rear blade release. The #11 blade included is an excellent cutting edge for most jobs.

First, select a piece of hardwood for the handle. The knife featured has a walnut handle, but almost any attractive and carvable wood is acceptable. A $^{21}\!/_{64}$"-diameter hole needs to be drilled through the length of the wood to accept a piece of tubing. For safety's sake, I recommend using a drill press and an oversized block that can be held in a clamp. This allows for a more accurately drilled hole, and there is less likelihood of breaking through the sides of the block. If you don't have a drill press, make sure you drill straight into the wood while not forcing the drill bit. Drill through the entire block until the bit exits.

With the block cut to 1" x ¾" wide x 3⅞" long, trace the pattern, onto the wood and cut it to shape using a coping, band, or scroll saw. Cut a piece of ⁵⁄₁₆" O.D. brass tubing—available in most craft and hardware stores—to 3⅞" in length. Mix enough five-minute epoxy to glue the tubing inside the handle. Coat the outside of the tubing with the epoxy and gently slide the tubing into the wood. Turn the tubing to spread the epoxy. If you accidentally get epoxy into the tubing, don't panic. Wait until it hardens slightly and use a drill bit to clean out the excess. Set the assembly aside until the epoxy has dried. About 15 minutes will ensure a good bond.

Using a rasp, file, or power-sanding device, round the sharp corners of the handle. Make sure you don't take away the contours and curves. Progressively sand the handle with 120-, 220-, and 400-grit sandpaper to achieve a smooth surface. Apply your favorite finish. Wax, varnish, lacquer, or an oil will all work well on the wood.

Disassemble the hobby knife, making sure the blade is safely set aside. Gently pry the end cap—a small piece of metal on the blade end—off the knife. Push the end cap into the front end of the handle using a vise or clamp. If there is a slip nut, make sure it is on the rear blade release. Insert the blade release assembly into the rear of the handle. Place the threaded end of the slotted blade grip into the end cap and gently turn the blade release to start the threads. Place the blade into the blade grip and finish tightening. You will have a knife sure to draw praise from fellow carvers.

Materials & Tools

Materials:
- 1" x ¾" x 3⅞" hardwood block
- ⁵⁄₁₆" O.D. x 3⅞" long brass tubing
- Five-minute epoxy
- Wax, varnish, lacquer, or oil finish

Tools:
- X-Acto Gripster Knife or similar
- Drill with ²¹⁄₆₄" drill bit
- Coping, band, or scroll saw
- Rasp, file, or power sanding device
- 120-, 220-, and 400-grit sandpaper

Assembly

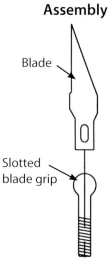

Blade

Slotted
blade grip

End cap

Slip nut
(if needed)

Rear blade
release

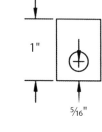

²¹⁄₆₄"

1"

⁵⁄₁₆"

Front

Top

Side

²¹⁄₃₂"

⁷⁄₈"

3⅞"

~¾"

¾"

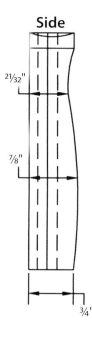

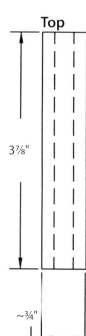

**Full-Size Pattern
for Handle**

Photocopy at 100%

⁵⁄₁₆"

Rear

3⅞"

3⅞"

**Brass Craft
Tubing**

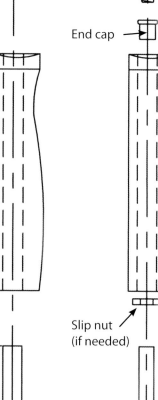

Custom-Made Knife Handles

I put a significant amount of effort into developing a knife handle that fit comfortably in my hand. I wanted to ensure a consistent result when I made new handles, so I traced the pattern from my drawn sketch onto .015"-thick clear plastic using a permanent ink pen. I trimmed the plastic to the edge of the pattern. Then, I used the trimmed plastic as a template for tracing the profile onto wood. Now, I can use this pattern over and over and obtain consistent results. There's no need to use a transfer medium, such as carbon paper, and the pattern is a heavy plastic that's less likely to get torn or creased.

Bob Langan
Edison, NJ

Stay-Tight Blade Cover

Many people make their own blade covers, but a reoccurring problem is that the covers slip off! To solve that, take a piece of wood and trace the shape of the knife blade onto it. Carve out the wood until the blade fits fully into the outline. On another piece of wood, mark the outline of the knife again. Mark and carve a recess for a small magnet of your choice. Glue the two pieces of wood together. The magnet will hold the cover in place!

Leonard Wovna
Belleville, NJ

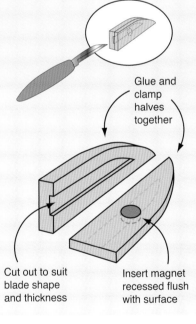

Glue and clamp halves together

Cut out to suit blade shape and thickness

Insert magnet recessed flush with surface

Tool Sheath

I am a mechanic and an amateur woodcarver. I recycle the plastic containers that oil comes in and make sheaths for my carving tools. Each sheath requires a 6"–8"-long strip of plastic and three wire ties.

Hyung Jun-Yong
Gyeonggi-do, South Korea

1 **Fold the strip in half.** Then, fold the ends toward the center fold.

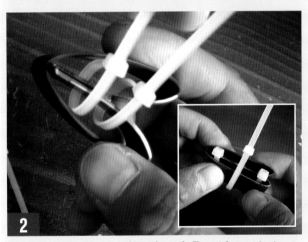

2 **Tighten two wire ties around just the ends.** Then, tighten a wire tie around the outside fold.

3 **Slide your tools into place.**

The V-tool:
No Carver Should Be Without One

By John Mignone

Photography by Roger Schroeder

The V-tool is one of the most useful tools a carver can own. Making V-type cuts by any other means is both time consuming and difficult.

The typical function of the V-tool is to separate one area from another. Although a gouge can perform the same function, it is the V-tool that leaves a wall and not a valley between one feature of a carving and another.

V-tools come in a variety of shapes and sizes. From top to bottom: straight, long bent, and short bent.

Getting a Grip on It

A V-tool, having two chisel-like sides called wings, is held like any other carving tool when you're not using a mallet. If you are right-handed, the left hand grips the tool just above the ferrule and down over the blade, while the thumb is placed against the handle. The grip should not be so tight it reduces left-hand flexibility. The rest of the handle is held with the pushing right hand. Reverse the positions for left-handers.

The heel of the gripping hand should always sit on the project. Change direction by bending the wrist in the direction you want the tool to go, using the side of the heel as a pivot. Keep the elbows close to the body and swing with the cut as you go around curves. Lower the handle to create shallower cuts and raise it for deeper cuts. When cutting, keep the corners of the tool out of the wood to prevent tearing the grain. You should also learn to swap hands if you need to carve in the opposite direction. The change of hands eliminates having to turn the wood or having to walk around it.

Good exercises include carving with the grain, carving across the grain, and making curves. Tight curves should be cut shallow to prevent the tool from chattering and creating an irregular surface.

Except for cross-grain cuts, the V-tool has one side cutting with the grain and the other side against it. Make sure the wing of the tool cutting with the grain is facing the area being separated from the rest of the carving. If the other wing tears wood, you can clean it up by reversing the tool's direction and cutting with the grain. Make sure the tool is held at an angle so it doesn't touch the area being separated.

Beginner Tool Sets

By Roger Schroeder

How many tools does a beginning carver need? Early records suggest that Medieval carvers had as many as 3,000 carving tools—and I know two contemporary carvers who do ornamental, architectural, and sculptural work and own between 200 and 300 tools each. However, the number of tools they use on a regular basis is probably less than 24.

How many standard chisels, gouges, and V-tools do you need to start out? Most companies offer hundreds of tools, far in excess of what will get you launched as a woodcarver. While a few will help remove wood in every conceivable shape or position, it's impossible to predict how wide your first tools should be. The size of your project will dictate the scale, but carvings change dimensions on a regular basis. If your projects are larger than caricature size, I suggest you look for tools between ½" and ¾" wide. Caricature carvers usually use smaller tools—about ¼" wide.

A suggested list for a starter set, based on recommendations I gathered in the field, appears in the chart at right. I also advise that you purchase a set of palm tools. While exceptional sets are offered by many companies, I'm reluctant to recommend one brand over another. I do suggest you evaluate the sizes offered. Sets include as few as six tools and as many as 12. If you can build a comfort zone with these sets, then it's time to branch out and get a feel for additional profiles and shapes.

Stubai designed this set to be used for all types of carving, including relief carving, statues, decorative, sign carving, figure carving, or roughing work for your small hand tools. This set includes a #3 12mm gouge, a #3 20mm gouge, a #9 12mm gouge, a #9 20mm gouge, and an 8mm V-tool.

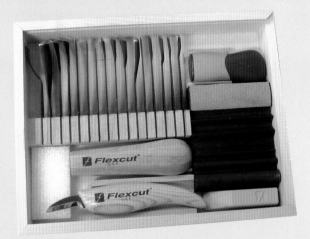

Flexcut offers a variety of chisel profiles that fit into one of two handles. The set includes a ⁵⁄₁₆" single-bevel straight chisel, a ⁹⁄₁₆" double-bevel skew chisel, a #3 ¼" gouge, a #3 ⅞" gouge, a #5 ½" gouge, a #6 ½" gouge, a #8 ¼" gouge, a #8 ⅜" gouge, a #8 ¹¹⁄₁₆" gouge, a #9 ⁹⁄₁₆" gouge, a #11 ¹⁄₁₆" gouge, a #11 ³⁄₁₆" thumbnail gouge, a #11 ½" thumbnail gouge, a ⁵⁄₃₂" 45° V-tool, a ⅜" 70° V-tool, a ⅞" back-bent gouge, a carving knife, and a Flexcut SlipStrop with honing compound.

——	chisel
⟍	skew chisel
‿	#3 gouge
⌣	#5 gouge
⋃	#8 gouge
⋁	#11 veiner
V	60° V-tool

UJ Ramelson's beginner set includes a #9 ⁵⁄₁₆" gouge, a shallow ⁹⁄₆₄" U-gouge, a ⁹⁄₆₄" bent V-tool, a ⅜" skew chisel, two carving knives (not shown), sharpening stones, honing oil, and a beginner's carving book.

Robert Sorby developed two different carving sets. The six-piece set, which includes a 10mm skew chisel, a #4 13mm gouge, a #5 6mm gouge, a #7 3mm gouge, a bent #7 10mm gouge, and a 3mm V-tool, is designed for beginners. The 12-piece set, designed for advanced carvers, also includes a 10mm straight chisel, a 3mm skew chisel, a #4 6mm gouge, a #4 19mm gouge, a #5 3mm gouge, a #5 13mm gouge, a #6 10mm gouge, a #8 19mm gouge, a #11 1.5mm gouge, a bent #5 19mm gouge, a short-bent #5 10mm gouge (spoon gouge), and a 6mm V-tool.

To properly hold a V-tool, grip right above the ferrule and down the blade. Make sure the heel of the gripping hand rests on the wood.

If you learn to swap hands so that you can carve in the opposite direction, you won't have to turn the project or walk around it.

Buying the Right Tool

There are two ways to measure a V-tool. One is the angle defined by the separation between the wings. Most V-tools are available with 45˚, 60˚, or 90˚ angles. Some companies, such as Pfeil, make a 35˚ tool. And one maker of custom-made woodcarving tools offers V-tools from 24˚ to 90˚. The other measurement is the distance from the tip of one wing to the tip of the another, which is in millimeters for most V-tools. Good sizes to begin carving with are 8mm to 12mm. The 60˚ V-tool has the greatest amount of applications and is used by most professional carvers.

When it comes to shapes, there are three available: straight, long bent, and short bent. The last two are best suited for carving in hollowed areas.

A good bevel for the V-tool's cutting edge is about 20˚. It can be slightly more for hardwoods and slightly less for softwoods, but 20˚ should work for most species of wood you want to carve.

When choosing a V-tool, buy from a quality manufacturer. Retailers, such as Woodcraft and The Japan Woodworker, will guarantee a properly heat-treated tool. Purchasing cheap V-tools will only result in frustration when trying to maintain a keen edge.

Keep a checklist in mind when selecting a V-tool. Be certain the inside of the V-groove is straight and in line with the handle. Make sure both wings have equal thickness. Look to see that the V-groove is directly in

Uses for Foam

Storing knives and protecting blades, especially when you have a large collection of carving tools, can be challenging. Blades will poke through canvas pouches, and wooden protectors are cumbersome and take up valuable space in your toolbox.

For a simple carving knife blade protector, take a piece of 2mm-thick craft foam available in 9" x 12" sheets in the craft departments of many retailers, and cut it to the size of the knife blade. Cut a front and back, both the same size, allowing approximately ¼" to ⅜" excess around all sides for gluing. Hot glue all around the edge of the bottom half except where the knife blade will lie and place the blade in the center of the bottom half. Carefully set the top half on the bottom half and press both halves together.

With a permanent marker, label the protector to identify which one goes with which blade. The foam provides for nonslip, lightweight protection and doesn't take up a lot of space.

Take any scraps of foam that you have left from the sheet and save them to replace the worn foam backing on your cushioned, sleeveless drum sander. Attach the foam to the mandrel using double-sided tape.

Ed Livingston
Pinellas Park, FL

V-tools can be purchased with very narrow cutting angles. This tool, custom-made by Charles Berold, has an angle of 24° and produces a fine line.

Comfortable Carving

Many of my older carving tools, such as chisels, gouges, veiners, and V-tools, have straight wooden handles of various lengths that are palm-pushed for detail work. In time, this becomes uncomfortable and blister forming. I found my solution while staying overnight in a hotel room. I spotted the individual shampoo and lotion containers the hotel provides. The quarter-size, ball-shaped, screw-on caps are perfect to place on the end of my tools.

Wrap masking tape around the palm end of the carving tool until the bottle cap fits firmly. Screw the cap in place, and you have an instant palm tool.

Dan Vetesk
Northport, AL

the middle and not offset. And, examine the walls of the V-tool. They should be relatively thin with each having the same thickness.

The V-tool is especially useful when creating special effects such as hair, fur, or feathers. It can even be used to make simple line drawings. Coat a light-colored wood with a dark, non-penetrating stain, such as a gel stain or a coat of latex paint, and carve through the coating. The results can be impressive.

Protecting Your Tools

Here's a tip for protecting knife blades, gouges, and other tools. Spray WD 40 on blades and wipe off any excess. Then, dip them into Plasti Dip, a rubber coating material used to insulate hand tools, such as pliers. You can find Plasti Dip at many home centers.

Dip the tools into the material several times to get the desired thickness. Once you loosen the rubber at the handle it is easy to pull the blade out. Use your custom sheath to protect your blades when not in use.

You can also coat the plastic tubing that many people use to protect their blades. Put some cloth or tissue in one end and dip it ¼" into the Plasti Dip. This will keep the blade from coming out.

Jack Simpson Sr.

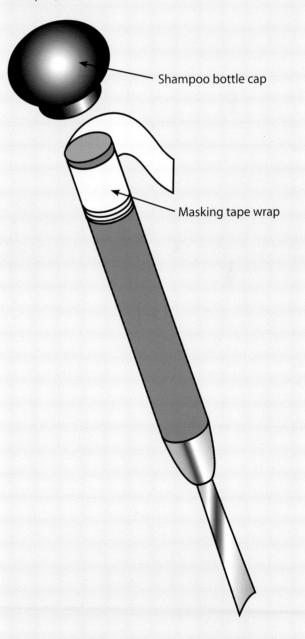

Shampoo bottle cap

Masking tape wrap

Disposable Blade
Carving Tools

By Bob Duncan

The most difficult part of carving for a beginner isn't removing wood—it's getting the tools sharpened and polished properly. There is nothing more frustrating than struggling with dull tools. In fact, it's probably the main reason many novice carvers don't continue the hobby. Thanks to the variety of disposable blades available, hobby carvers can enjoy the creative side of woodcarving without the tedium of sharpening.

Disposable blades will never replace a professional carver's tools, but many hobby

carvers prefer the freedom from sharpening. When a blade dulls, you can replace it with a new one. Some carvers strop the disposable blades on a leather strop and replace the blade only when it would require reshaping with a stone or grinder. Disposable blades are also nice for RVers, campers, or travelers because they are compact and don't require you to pack sharpening equipment.

Many manufacturers offer the traditional triangular-shaped hobby knife, but several manufacturers are making a limited selection of blade, chisel, and gouge profiles for carvers.

X-Acto

X-Acto began manufacturing a variety of scalpel blades with a unique handle that accommodated all of their blade shapes in the 1930s. The classic triangular shape of the blade was based on a sketch by an advertising artist who needed a knife for retouching photographs. This distinct shape, which was marketed to artists and hobbyists as the X-Acto #11 blade, set the industry standard.

Disposable blades are a low-maintenance, low-cost option for beginner carvers.

Disposable Blade Pros and Cons

Benefits of Disposable Blades:

- Are inexpensive and require a minimal investment in tools
- Offer the convenience of easy storage when traveling
- Eliminate the need for sharpening equipment and skills
- Are an ideal way for beginners to explore the hobby of woodcarving without a large investment of time or money

Drawbacks of Disposable Blades:

- Are not as durable as fixed-blade carving tools
- Are only available in limited sizes and profiles

Comparison of Popular Disposable Blades

Brand	Material	Use	Replacement Blades	Beginner Set	Availability	Highlights
X-Acto	Stainless Steel	General use, tips can be fragile and may break if you try to remove too much wood	$0.30 (simple blades) to $1.50 (specialty blades)	$20	Widely available at department and grocery stores	Available in a variety of profiles including gouges, V-tools, and chisels
Warren Cutlery	High-carbon Steel	General use, blades tend to be thicker and more durable	$1 to $1.75 (simple blades) to $10 (specialty blades)	$20-$75	Available at woodworking supply stores	Handle is specifically designed for carvers
Excel	High-carbon Steel	General use, tips can be fragile and may break if you try to remove too much wood	$0.25 (simple blades) to $1 (specialty blades)	$20	Available at hobby stores	Interchangeable with X-Acto blades and handles
Veritas Carvers' Knife	Stainless steel	Detail carving, thin scalpels can snap easily, not recommended for roughing out a carving	$0.15 for most profiles	$29.50	Available through Lee Valley and at surgical supply stores	Blades can be stored in the handle for easy travel

Other common brand names of disposable blade systems include Zona, Stanley, Ace, and Testors, which are similar in quality and price to X-Acto.

The primary advantage of the now ubiquitous triangular X-Acto blades is their vast availability and low cost. You can find packages of 100 blades for around $30. They are sharp and thin enough to remove wood quickly, but they do not stay sharp as long as a carbon steel carving knife. You also have to be careful not to break off the thin fragile tip. The standard handles can be difficult to use for long periods of time.

X-Acto launched a tool division for the hobby market in the 1960s, and since then, the company has developed a product line specifically for woodcarvers. In addition to fixed blade woodcarving tools, X-Acto created a line of disposable blades for carving. The kits include gouges, V-tools, chisels, scorps (which they call routers), and knife blades. Some of the tool profiles are available separately.

The handle that comes with the kit (shown ar right) is larger than the standard handle, but it still lets you change the blades without using a wrench or special tool. The larger handle is much more comfortable for most woodcarving purposes.

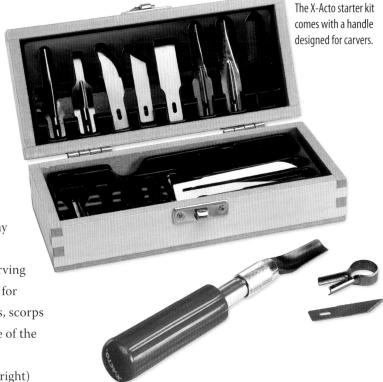

The X-Acto starter kit comes with a handle designed for carvers.

Veritas Carver's Knife

The Veritas Carver's Knife, available from Lee Valley, is designed to use standard scalpel blades. Scalpel blades are thin, so they will snap if you apply pressure from the side. A box of 100 scalpel blades is less than $15.

The primary advantage of the Veritas Carver's Knife is you can store up to six blades in the handle. The handle can be slipped into a pocket or purse easily.

Excel Hobby Blades

Excel Hobby Blades haven't been around as long as X-Acto and Warren Cutlery, but they produce affordable durable blades. Overall, the Excel blades are similar in shape and function to X-Acto, but they are made from high-carbon steel and stay sharp longer.

Excel handles are similar to X-Acto and you can switch back and forth between Excel and X-Acto blades using the same handle. Excel blades can be hard to find. They are available at most hobby stores. Boxes of 100 standard blades can be purchased for around $25 and assortment packs of specially shaped blades and gouges are less than $3 a package. Excel also offers scorp (router) profiles.

Warren Cutlery

Warren Tools feature interchangeable disposable blades that clamp in a handle. The high-carbon steel blades come in a variety of sizes and shapes, including chisel and gouge profiles.

Warren offers several handle shapes, including a traditional knife handle, a version shaped more like a palm tool handle, and one made with an easy-to-grip rubber coating. Each Warren handle comes with a custom wrench that allows you to tighten the blades firmly into the handle. A package of three blades runs between $3 and $5, depending on the size. This is more expensive than other disposable blades, but the high-carbon steel holds an edge longer.

The chisel and gouge profiles are more expensive. Most average around $10, which falls outside the disposable category for many carvers. The gouges fit into some, but not all, of Warren's handles.

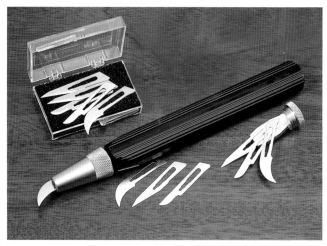

You can store up to 6 blades in the handle of the Veritas Carver's Knife.

Excel blades are made of durable high-carbon steel.

The Warren Cutlery kit includes a variety of useful blade profiles.

All About
Mallets

By Roger Schroeder

A good mallet, whether made from solid wood or synthetic materials, is an essential companion to hand tools such as chisels and gouges.

If you're not a power or chip carver, and whittling wood with a knife doesn't cut it for you, then chisels, gouges, and V-tools are most likely your tools of choice. While much wood removal can be accomplished with just hand power, eventually another tool joins in: the mallet.

My first carvings were deep relief, and whacking away wood with vigor was the game plan. Hand tools with fancy rosewood handles adorned my workbench, and the mallet that propelled chisels, gouges, and V's through the wood was a clunky, square-faced brute made from beech—I called it the enforcer. Now with severely dented faces, it hangs on a pegboard in my shop, a warrior put to rest, though still admired for fights it won against the hardest of woods.

Back then in my novice days of woodcarving—it would be generous at present to call myself an intermediate carver—I did not realize a mallet with a flat face is meant for cutting woodworking joints, not for carving projects!

A typical woodworking joint is a mortise, which is a square-faced hole. The woodworker's chisel, which has a bevel on one side of the blade, is the preferred tool, and it must be struck squarely to guide it as precisely as possible. When using a carver's chisel, which has a bevel on both sides, a gouge, or a V, you end up striking the tool from a variety of directions because you are likely to approach wood removal from almost any angle that is comfortable, and probably from some that are not. A round head offers easier control for propelling edge tools through wood using either direct or oblique blows.

It's a chip at a time with hand tools for wood sculptor Armand LaMontagne. But a custom-made mallet from white oak burl and a sharp gouge rough-shaped this life-size sculpture in a matter of weeks.

The Mallet Ballot

The typical carver's mallet has two prominent features: a round head and a handle with some contour for better gripping. I tested eight different mallets, and there were more differences than similarities. Be aware that hand, arm muscle, bone, and nerve ailments are always a problem, no matter how well you choose your tools (see sidebar, page 85). Here's what I found.

Lignum Vitae

Lignum vitae mallets have been popular with carvers for decades. A dense, oily wood that weighs in at 88 pounds per cubic foot when dry, it packs a punch. In one reference to the wood, I read that lignum vitae's resistance to denting was ranked first out of 405 wood species tested. A problem with the mallets I examined is they often check, although the cracks are usually surface ones and the integrity of the mallet is not diminished. However, checks can catch your clothing or, worse, the skin of your hand. Lignum vitae is a tropical hardwood found throughout the Caribbean and Central America. If you do purchase a lignum vitae mallet, you'll likely find it coated with wax to slow down the checking that occurs when the wood enters the drier climates of the north.

The lignum vitae tree is a slow grower. I have seen these trees flourishing in the Florida Keys, and 1,000-year-old specimens were no more than a foot in diameter. Unfortunately, lignum vitae may be the victim of over-harvesting, as so many tropical woods are. If you find yourself allied with Save the Rainforest or you are just plain environmentally conscious, this may not be the mallet for you.

Tonca

Another mallet I checked out is tonca wood. Often sold as a substitute for lignum vitae, it is not as dense as its tropical cousin, meaning it will likely wear out sooner, but it seems to resist checking. The mallet I purchased has a rounded bottom, a feature that makes it easy to stand the tool on a workbench without having it fall over. Standing a mallet upright is always the best way to put it aside. If you lay it down, it will probably roll off the bench. The tonca wood mallet is one piece, as is the typical lignum vitae mallet, and it should last for a good while with moderate use.

Lignum vitae is an excellent wood for a mallet because it is heavy, dense, and very resistant to denting.

Tonca wood is a tropical hardwood that makes for an excellent mallet. The bottom of this mallet is slightly rounded, which makes it easy to stand upright—the only position the tool should be in.

Beech

European carvers seem fond of beech mallets. While not as dense as lignum vitae—dry weight is 43 pounds per cubic foot—a beech mallet is a rugged tool that should withstand years of pounding because of its ability to withstand shock. I'm delighted with the one I own because it has a hickory handle. Hickory is noted for its resilience and resistance to bone-jarring impacts. If you need proof of that, look at vintage wooden wagon wheels and appreciate they're still around. Some of their components were made from this species.

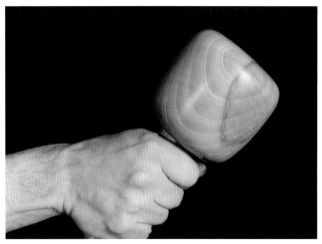

A mallet made from beech is extremely shock resistant, especially if it has a hickory handle, as this one does.

Lignostone

One company went a step further with beech and turned it into Lignostone. A Lignostone mallet is made from beech laminations. Applied perpendicularly to the face of the mallet, the laminations are bonded using thermosetting synthetic resins under high pressure. Made in the Netherlands, these mallets have a density five times greater than solid beech and twice the elasticity. It's reassuring to know the distributor guarantees the material will not crack or chip. Lignostone mallets are expensive. An entry-level solid beech mallet costs about $20. A Lignostone mallet of the same weight costs more than twice that. I purchased one that weighs 36 oz. It has a good feel and makes quick work of wood removal. I tried it on Jamaican dogwood, an extremely hard tropical wood, and I was pleased with the results. Will it live up to its reputation? Only time will tell, but I'm betting it will be around long after I've carved my last piece.

Lignostone is made from layers of beech veneer, bonded together under high pressure with a synthetic resin.

Oak Burl

An all-wood mallet I had custom-made has a head made from oak burl. A burl is a growth on a tree that has grain growing in aberrant patterns. Oak burl is both dense and rugged. When used as a mallet, it compresses and becomes even more durable. It's a favorite tool with realistic wood sculptor Armand LaMontagne, and being familiar with his creations, I did not need much convincing that an oak burl mallet would make an excellent wood removal facilitator. Making one is not difficult if you have a lathe (see illustration on page 85).

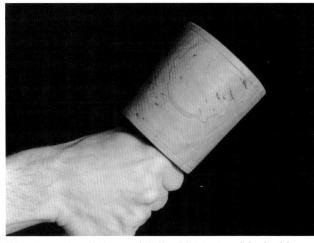

This custom-made mallet has an oak burl head that is extremely hard and dense.

Hard Carving Mallet

Technology keeps changing not only automobiles and satellites but also mallets. I'm particularly impressed with a so-called hard head carving mallet I acquired. With an ultra-wear, polyethylene head and maple handle, this mallet's strengths include its indestructible head. You can recognize one from 100' away because of its white head. Not subject to cracking or wear, this mallet is truly a lifetime investment. However, I could acquire only a 16-oz. size, and that's a little too light for the carving I do on some very hard species of wood. But I chipped away with the mallet and found it comfortable to use, and the cutting tool handles left hardly a scratch on the head.

Quiet Carving Mallet

Another quality innovation is the quiet carving mallet. Like the hard head, it is guaranteed unbreakable, although this one is made from a tough urethane material designed to be—what else?—quiet. Complete with a maple handle, the mallet is available in four sizes—12, 18, 20 and 30 oz. I purchased the largest size and worked at removing wood from an oak relief panel. Not only did the mallet deliver a good, solid blow, but it also transmitted little shock to my arm. I've heard carvers swear this tool is the solution to elbow stress. It's definitely worth having in your arsenal of wood removers.

Metal Head

A mallet that is becoming more popular in the United States is the variety with a metal head. Small in size, the head is either lead-iron alloy, sometimes called a dummy mallet, or bronze. With the mass concentrated in the compact head, the mallet delivers a blow with no rebound, so there is a reduced likelihood of wrist, forearm, and elbow stress. The one I use, a bronze-headed mallet, has a good heft and does not require a crushing blow to the cutting tool. In fact, I can limit my motion to a simple wrist pivot. When using this type of mallet, I do recommend gripping it with the thumb positioned on the back of the head for better control.

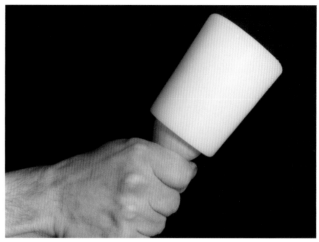

The hard head mallet, made from polyethylene, is virtually indestructible.

The quiet mallet should reduce the problems of stress to the elbow and hand.

This bronze-headed mallet offers a solid blow with little rebound. The best grip is with the thumb behind the head and rest of the fingers wrapped around the head.

Is a Mallet for You?

Not yet familiar with mallet carving but interested in breaking the ice? Before purchasing a mallet, go to a woodworking or an art supply store that carries sculptors' tools and heft what is available. While only an extended period of carving time will tell if the tool is right for you, at least get a feel for what it's going to be like to hold a mallet. Once I passed the holding test, I discovered after carving for a day that a 24- to 26-oz. mallet is about right for me. I can manage a 34-oz. mallet for a shorter period of time without too much stress on my body, but anything heavier is meant for a weight lifter, not a 153-pound writer-photographer. I also realized that having a small hand—mine measures 4" from the wrist to the base of the fingers—requires a handle that is not too big in diameter. Every mallet I tried out has a different size handle, and some are a tad too large for me. While a lathe can reduce the size, that is not easy to do on many mallets owing to their synthetic or metal construction.

Making Your Own Mallet

A custom mallet can require some experimentation and failures. Even estimating how heavy the end result will be can be problematic. If you want to give it a try, a mallet can be turned, even carved, from one piece of wood, but the material you use for the head may not be right for the handle. Oak is not good to grip because it is splintery, but oak burl is ideal for a head. Or, perhaps you found a chunk of a very suitable hardwood, but not enough to lend itself to head and handle.

To make a two-piece mallet on a lathe, the head and handle are turned separately. A hole is drilled into the bottom of the head—at least halfway, but more is preferable—and the end of the handle is reduced in size. The resulting tenon is slightly smaller than the hole in the head. Make a kerf cut with a saw in the tenon for the insertion of a narrow wedge of wood. As you pound the handle into the mallet, the wedge spreads the tenon to create a force fit. Do not apply an adhesive if the handle is not tightly seated—meaning a snug fit— in the head. A glue joint will most likely fail and cause injury.

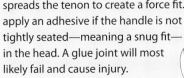

Does Any Mallet Offer the Perfect Rx?

You don't have to be a physician to appreciate that conditions with the names "cumulative trauma disorder" and "hand-arm syndrome" spell trouble. The first includes ailments of the tendons, nerves, bones, and muscles associated with hand-arm vibration disorders involving considerable use of the upper arm. Symptoms include pain and impairment of the upper arm. The second, also known as "dead man's hand," results from hand-arm vibration over many years and can lead to reduced gripping strength.

If using a mallet produces any symptoms of pain, numbness, limited hand or arm use, tingling, or temperature sensitivity, stop using the tool.

Mallets at a Glance

	Pros	Cons
Lignum vitae	Packs a punch, tops for dent resistance	Often checks or cracks
Tonca wood	Resists checking	May not hold up with frequent and heavy use
Beech	Rugged tool, able to withstand shock	A separate handle could come loose
Lignostone	Durable and extremely dense	Pricey
Oak burl	Becomes more durable with use	Limited availability
Hard head	Indestructible	Limited sizes
Quiet	Reduces arm trauma	Large-diameter handle may be uncomfortable
Metal head	No rebound, good heft	Typically expensive; small size can take getting used to

Still Having Problems?

Here's a short list of possible problems you might have with mallet use and some problem-solving tips:

- Problem: Your wooden mallet is starting to check.
- Solution: Store the mallet in a plastic bag with a damp rag or wet wood chips.
- Problem: You feel fatigued after a short period of mallet carving.
- Solution: Slow your pace of wood removal. Evaluate whether you have your body weight behind the mallet with the elbow of the mallet-holding hand close to the body.

All About
Files, Rasps, and Rifflers

Files come in a variety of profiles and sizes. They can remove wood quickly or produce a smooth surface.

By Roger Schroeder

While purists will argue that files, rasps, and rifflers, not to mention sandpaper, should never touch a woodcarving, don't sell these tools short. Many projects need a smooth surface, not a flat-plane or faceted one. These versatile tools can shape, smooth, even sharpen if necessary, and are actually economical alternatives to sandpaper. They are ideally suited for working oddly shaped areas and difficult wood grain, as well as roughing out. A single file removes wood as quickly as a large rotary cutter and produces a finished surface rivaling 220-grit sandpaper for smoothness.

Files

A file has three main parts: the length, which is the cutting surface covered with teeth; the tang, which is where the handle is attached (never use the tang as a handle); and the heel, which is the transition between the length and the tang. Files come in a wide variety of types and profiles.

Types of files: You need to understand both the cut of the teeth, that look like lines, and how coarse or smooth a finish they make. From coarse to smooth, the distance between the teeth diminishes. However, a smaller file has teeth closer together, even if it is labeled coarse. In general, the longer the file, the coarser it is. To help the consumer, manufacturers often stamp the cut between the first row of teeth and the tang.

File profiles: Once you've determined what type of file is best suited for the job, you can further refine the usefulness of the tool by selecting the correct profile or shape.

Rasps

Rasps make deeper and coarser cuts than files because they have separate and triangular, rather than parallel, lines of teeth. Rasps scrape away wood rather than plane it away as files do. The rasp is well suited for shaping wood quickly. Files have gullets or spaces between the teeth that fill with wood chips. One advantage a rasp has over a file is the teeth resist clogging, but rasps are only available in a limited variety. The size and distribution of teeth determine a rasp's degree of coarseness and the amount of wood it can remove. All cut rapidly but will leave a rough surface. Over the years, files and rasps have evolved into more specialized tools, such as rifflers, Microplane rasps, and needle files.

Rifflers and Specialized Tools

Riffler comes from a French word meaning to file or scrape. A riffler is a small, double-ended file, rasp, or both, with a gripping area between the cutting edges. It is fashioned to work in tight spaces. Common end shapes include straight, curved, and knife-like. Rifflers come in a variety of profiles, such as oval, triangular, square, round, and half-round.

Needle files are designed for very precise work and leave a smooth surface. A good set will consist of as many as 12 second-cut files, but purchase one that offers an interchangeable handle.

Rifflers give you access to tight areas.

At a Glance

Files, Rasps, and Rifflers:

- Take over where other tools leave off
- Ensure a straight cut due to the rigidity of the tools
- Shear impartially through alternating hard and soft grain
- Require only a light touch
- Require no sharpening
- Are widely available and relatively inexpensive
- Are capable of a wide variety of wood removal techniques

Microplane's stainless steel blades, which come in round, triangular, and flat shapes, offer razor-sharp edges. I tried my flat-blade Microplane on a piece of white oak and was more than pleased with the results. For the power carver, there are 1" and 2"-diameter rotary cutters with ¼" shanks. These tools should be used on a drill press running at a maximum of 1,200 rpm, not in a hand drill or flexible shaft tool.

Using Files and Rasps

Draw filing, a finishing stroke, requires you to hold the file in both hands at right angles to the wood and push across it with light pressure. Since the teeth of files cut only on the push stroke, lift the tool up on the return stroke. A beginner's problem is overdoing the push stroke operation, resulting in an unwanted hollow.

Cross filing is done at an angle, not straight across as the name might suggest. Hold the file with both hands and apply enough pressure so the teeth do not catch on the wood grain and cause the file to skip over hard and soft grain changes. Working at an angle is critical when using rasps. Filing parallel or perpendicular to the grain will tear and break the wood, leaving the surface ragged, with a lot of follow-up work required. Cross filing will prevent that from happening.

Care and Maintenance

While files are made from ultra-hard steel and tempered hard to give the teeth a long life, they do tend to be brittle and are easily broken. Files are not designed to pry, hammer, or clash with other metal tools. Use them for what they were designed for, and they should last several lifetimes.

Keep files hanging up and away from other tools. If wall space is at a premium, then keep them stored, but separated, in a drawer to protect the teeth. Since files, like most other steel implements, are prone to rust, it's wise to keep a few bags of silica in the drawer to draw off moisture.

A file card is the best investment you can make for unclogging a file that has filled with wood chips. Purchase one that has nylon bristles on one side and short, stiff steel teeth on the other. Badly clogged files require you to brush the file with the steel teeth. Stroke the brush parallel to the file's teeth. If you want to prevent heavy clogging, use the bristle brush frequently. If you chalk the teeth heavily prior to use, it will discourage clogging. Do not oil a file; it will make it difficult to dislodge dust and wood chips.

File Types

Name	Use
Single-cut	Precision work
Double-cut	Fast wood removal
Coarse	Fast wood removal
Bastard	Medium-fast wood removal
Second	Medium wood removal
Smooth	Slow wood removal, smooth surface

File Profiles

Profile	Use
Mill	Smoothing large curves or flat areas
Half-Round	Roughing out or shaping large inside curves
Triangular	Tight areas or hard to reach spots
Rat-tail	Shaping or enlarging holes, or shaping tight inside curves
Square	Shaping inside corners
Chainsaw	Smoothing inside curves
Knife	Tight areas where clearance is a problem

Rasps

Name	Use
Flat bastard or flat wood rasp	Quick wood removal on flat surfaces
Half-round bastard or half-round wood rasp	Quick wood removal on flat or curved surfaces
Second cut or cabinet rasp	Medium wood removal
Smooth or patternmaker's rasp	Slower wood removal, produces a smoother surface

All About
Drawknives,
Spokeshaves, and Scorps

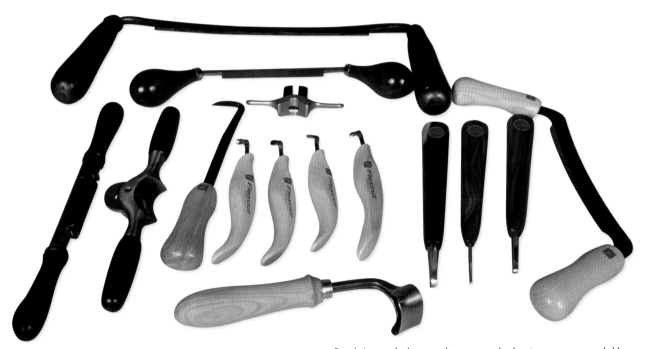

Drawknives, spokeshaves, and scorps open the door to some new—and old—ways of removing wood.

By Roger Schroeder

As a woodcarver, you know the game plan is to remove wood. A sharp knife can't be beat for a small project in softwoods. For large hardwood pieces, chisels, gouges, V-tools, and power tools get the job done accurately and efficiently. But other cutting tools such as drawknives, spokeshaves, and scorps are available. Despite their intimidating names, they have found their way into woodcarvers' shops.

The Drawknife

What is a drawknife? Visualize a two-handled chisel with a very long cutting edge and single bevel. The typical form offers a long naked blade tapering into narrow ends or tangs. To make the blade more manageable, the tangs are covered with wooden handles. Most handles are bent at angles to the blade, but a few come straight out. The drawknife can tackle both convex and concave surfaces, pare wood down exactly to a line, and hog off wood very quickly. If the blade is curved in, the drawknife becomes an inshave, which works great for hollowing out work.

Drawknives, Spokeshaves and Scorps at a Glance

Tool	Uses	Techniques
Drawknife	• Roughing out carvings • Shaving down to an exact line • Hollowing out concave surfaces • Cleaning up a convex surface	• Cuts on pull or push stroke • Bevel down for control • Bevel up to shave to a line • Extra bevel on back adds control
Spokeshave	• Smoothing rough surfaces • Rounding off carvings • Cleaning up tool marks	• Cuts on push or pull stroke • Works like handplane • Cuts fine shavings
Scorp	• Hollowing out concave surfaces • Roughing out inside surfaces • Cutting grooves	• Cuts on pull stroke • As fine a finish as a gouge • Cuts fine shavings

Is Using a Drawknife Safe?

I've heard of no serious mishaps with the drawknife, but be prudent. When you want to clear away chips, keep the tool well to one side so you don't sweep the clean-up hand into the blade. And don't work with your body too close to the project.

Sharpening

Because of the long blade and the handles, it's hard to sharpen a drawknife on a grinding wheel. For that reason, it's a good idea to purchase a new one that will probably need just a good honing and not a major sharpening.

If you do need to sharpen it, you have several options. The safest way is to hold the tool upright with one handle resting on a workbench or tabletop. Use a flat sharpening stone—diamond, ceramic, natural, and manmade are all good choices. Make sure the stone is flat against the bevel and apply long strokes instead of short choppy ones. Use an extra-fine stone on the back to get rid of the wire edge.

If you do manage to get a ding in the blade, or if it's one of those antiques dulled by years of neglect, then you are in for a little work. A fine mill file, available at most hardware stores and home improvement centers, works well to reshape the edge. It will take some time to get the bevel in tip-top shape, but the result will be worth the effort.

Some drawknife enthusiasts put a slight bevel on the back of the blade for extra maneuverability when working with the bevel up. There is more control with this extra bevel, but it is hard to grind or file evenly across the long cutting edge.

Spokeshaves

If you want to compare a spokeshave to a familiar tool, think handplane. New spokeshaves, designed with a cutter and cap iron, come in several shapes: flat-edge for flat and some round surfaces, half-round for convex cuts, radius for hollows, and chamfer for edges. Not all, however, are going to be useful in woodcarving.

Put to Use

A spokeshave can be pushed or pulled and leaves the same finish as a handplane. It's not an easy tool to use, but you can put a very smooth finish on a variety of surfaces. Keep in mind that the tool is not designed for hogging off wood. Aim to produce fine shavings.

Traditionally, the spokeshave was a furniture carver's tool used to shape curved legs and rolling skirts on tables and cabinets. But I find the tool ideal for removing facets prior to sanding the hardwood sculptures I like to carve. It's not a big investment to own one of these tools, and it will probably come in handy one day when you find your favorite carving tools can't achieve the surface you are looking for.

Get a Grip on It—8 Steps to Mastering the Drawknife

1. Take a good look at the drawknife and study its anatomy. Grip the tool firmly in both hands, but not too hard. Hold it so the bevel is up, then turn it around so the bevel is facing down. The tool should feel pretty much the same, regardless of which way the bevel is facing.

2. Prepare your practice block. Find a sizable chunk of scrap wood and clamp it firmly in a holding fixture. Make sure the area you are going to work on is fully exposed and fairly flat. Orient the wood so you can cut with the grain.

3. Practice cutting bevel-side down. Find a position that offers a firm, braced stance on the floor. Holding the tool bevel side down, pull or "draw" it toward you. If the tool is razor sharp, a chip or curl should break free from the surface almost immediately. Take a number of short and long strokes.

4. Practice cutting bevel-side up. Turn the tool over so the bevel side is up. Again, remove wood with a series of short and long strokes.

5. Refine the cuts. Hold the blade at an angle to the work, either bevel up or down, and slide the blade to one side as you pull the tool. It helps to imagine slicing a loaf of bread. Begin at a point about 1" from an edge and work to the opposite side.

6. Use your thumbs for more control. For more control, place your thumbs on the upper part of the blade and grip the handles with the rest of your fingers.

7. Master the push stroke. Turn the tool so that the cutting edge is facing away. With bevel up and then down, push the blade across the surface. This technique saves you from having to turn a project around if grain changes direction.

8. Practice heavy strokes for aggressive wood removal. With a good grip on the handles and the bevel down, make a series of short, heavy yanking strokes toward you. You should dig the blade into the wood and bring the handles up. Keep the blade angled to the surface and slide the blade from one side to the other.

After using the drawknife both ways, it's easy to see what the bevel does. With the bevel down, the tool tends to rise up from the cut. With the bevel side up, you can remove finer shavings and cut closer to a line.

When hollowing out a project with the drawknife, cut with the bevel down. As you pull or push, lightly lift the handles clear. Work to the low point from both sides of a concave surface to avoid breaking away too much wood.

When working on a convex surface, start at the high point of the curve and cut down. You can cut with the bevel side down, but if you cut with the bevel side up you can pare away the wood with a lot of control.

Sharpening and Care

The problem with sharpening a spokeshave's cutter is its size. The curved and radius profiles are difficult or impossible to put to a grinding wheel, and even the flat-edge cutter is hard to hold to a wheel without a holding fixture. My advice is to purchase a new blade if the one you are using gets too dull. However, if the blade only needs to be honed, a round honing stone works fine for curved blades and flat stones work for flat blades. That said, if your cutting edge does get a nick, replace it.

When not in immediate use, put the tool blade down on a wooden work surface. Don't worry about dulling the edge—it's meant for wood. Nothing dulls an edge faster than hitting it with another steel tool. Many spokeshaves have a hole in one handle, so hanging it up is a good storage option.

Spokeshave Tips

1. Grip the tool with both hands. Thumb pads are sometimes cast in the frame, so that's where your digits belong. It's the thumbs that push when moving the spokeshave forward and the other fingers steer.

2. Keep a good steady downward pressure on the tool. If you don't, it will chatter and skip.

3. Shearing action produces clean cuts. Once you make some passes with the tool, hold it at a slightly skewed angle to achieve a shearing action that produces a much cleaner cut.

Scorps

If an inshave works well, imagine how useful it would be if the blade were bent into a loop with both tangs fitted into one handle. Coopers and bowl makers have already been using this tool, a scorp, for many years. It hollows.

Sometimes called a single-hand inshave, the scorp definitely has a place among woodcarvers. With the bevel on the outside, it leaves as clean a finish as a gouge and usually works on the pull stroke. Scorps come in a variety of sizes. The largest are 4" across with a nearly 7" cutting edge. Micro scorps have openings as small as 1/16".

To use the tool, get a good grip on the handle, let the cutting edge dig into the wood, and give a pull. If the tool is well honed, it should take out a nice curl from basswood. Don't cut too deep at first. This tool is meant for light wood removal.

Sharpening Strategies

Scorps with large openings are easily sharpened with flat stones on the outside and round ones to hone off the burr on the inside. Micro scorps require a different strategy. To maintain a razor-sharp edge, use a honing compound or micron paper over a piece of flat glass. To remove the burr on the inside, use a short length of dowel slightly smaller than the opening. Wrap the dowel with fine sandpaper or charge it with honing compound. Push the dowel in from the top and hone away from the cutting edge.

What's New on the Market?

Aside from the micro scorps, which I find excellent for cleaning up small recesses, Flexcut Tools has come out with an innovative design. Instead of a complete circle, these small scorps are open on the top, with the cutting edge at right angles to the handle. Their profiles suggest gouges and V-tools. Like traditional scorps, they can be pulled and are available for both right- and left-hand use. If you feel comfortable changing hands, you can push the tool away from you. I tried out a set of four and enjoyed using all of them.

Drawknives, spokeshaves, and scorps may not be for every woodcarver. But when your best knife, chisel, gouge, V-tool, or rotary bit just can't do the job, then it's time to turn to one of these exceptional tools.

Scorp Tips

Frustration levels can reach the boiling point when working with new tools, and especially with harder woods. Set aside knot-free white pine scraps of different thicknesses to try out wood-shaping tools such as drawknives, spokeshaves, and scorps. When you get comfortable with the tools, then graduate to harder species.

A hollowing tool, the scorp can quickly scoop out wood.

When sharpening a large scorp, use a round hone to remove the burr on the inside.

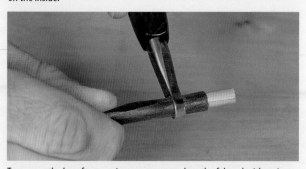

To remove the burr from a micro scorp, wrap a length of dowel with a piece of sandpaper or charge it with honing compound.

Check out the innovative Flexcut scorps that can be pulled or pushed through wood.

All About
Punches

By Roger Schroeder

Tap the steel punch with a hammer to leave a textured impression. Above, Chris Pye creates a textured background with a simple punch.

A woodcarver's punch is a steel texturing tool with a pattern engraved on its tip. Common designs consist of a single dot, a series of dots, an asterisk, or a cross shape. But don't be surprised to find letters, acorns, hearts, anchors, stars, and crescent moons, among others. To use it, place the punch perpendicular to the surface of the wood and strike it with a hammer. It's as simple as that.

Aside from the notion of a textured contrast, there are other reasons for using a punch. For one, it disguises a ragged background. Some species of wood, especially when relief carved, simply defy clean cuts where the grain changes. When hard-to-remove splinters show up in small crevices, the pros recommend you find a punch that fits in the space and compresses the wood.

Punches for Convex Effects

Instead of the design standing proud of the surface on a punch, the design can be recessed on the punch to create a convex shape on the wood. Eye punches were designed to compress the background so a round or oval mound is left. Punches can also be used to make scales and buttons.

One clever use of a punch is raising bumps. This technique is perfect for creating bumps on a frog.

- Find a piece of scrap basswood and a 10-penny nail.
- Tap the head of the nail on the surface of the scrap.
- Sand the punch mark until it has nearly disappeared.
- Put a few drops of boiling water on the compressed area and wait for a bump to appear.

When the walls of wood cells are disturbed, as in compression, they swell when wet. It's a trick furniture restorers use to remove dents.

Making a Punch

Dozens of different punches are available at reasonable prices. If you just can't find that pattern you've always wanted, try making the tool. Large 16-penny nails offer a lot of steel on which you can engrave a design using files or rotary bits. Another material to consider is steel mending plates. Created to join two pieces of wood or to strengthen a wood joint, the typical plate measures ⅝" x 3" and is ³⁄₃₂" thick. It's readily hammered and the steel is soft enough to file a design into. I've created patterns that simulate zippers, stitches, and weaving.

A simple circular punch can be made from a length of copper tubing. However, you should have a bevel on either the outside or inside, depending on the effect you want. Put the piece of tubing into a drill press and hold a small reamer to the inside as it rotates at low speed to quickly form an inside bevel. To achieve an outside bevel, hold a diamond hone to the spinning end of the tubing. For an oval shape, gently crimp the end with a pair of pliers.

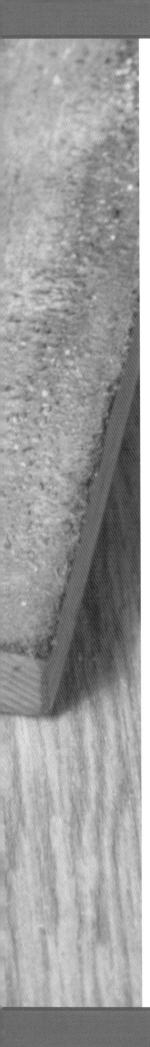

Sharpening

Sharpening is often considered one of the trickiest parts of woodcarving. After reading through this chapter, you'll have a solid foundation in the techniques required for sharpening your tools and keeping them in tip-top shape. Know you need a bench stone, but have no idea which one to select? Wondering whether there's a better way to sharpen your V-tool? Read on for the answers—and more.

Everything you need to know about sharpening, including stropping, is covered here.

Bench Stones

By John Mignone

I've been asked, especially by newcomers, to recommend the one bench stone they should purchase as a sharpening aid. Although this sounds like a simple question, it's not—a lot goes into bench stone selection. Does the carver use a knife and one or two palm tools, or does he/she carve with full-size chisels and gouges? Is a grinding wheel available? And with what regularity are the tools finely honed or sharpened? These answers help determine the types of bench stones the carver needs. This article should clear up some of your questions and help you select the bench stone that's right for you.

In the Beginning

The earliest edge tools were made from flint, which was chipped to form a hard edge. In the Bronze Age, tools were fashioned from copper and copper alloys. Edges were beaten to shape. When iron and steel tools came into vogue, an abrasive was required to refine and restore an edge.

In the history of abrasives, a naturally occurring material called sandstone was traditionally used to sharpen tools. Sandstone—sand being a description of particle size, not composition—came in two forms: bench stones and grinding wheels. Often rectangular in shape, the bench stone got its name because it was placed flat on a woodworker's or carver's bench and the cutting edge was moved across the stone's face.

While either bench stones, grinding wheels, or both are in almost every carver's shop, there have been some changes in the material and technology in the last century. Sandstone, consisting of naturally bonded quartz crystals, has been replaced. Man-made materials are commonly used today: these sharpening stones are composed of much harder but still-natural stones, held together with resinous bonding agents.

Advantages of a Bench Stone

- A good bench stone removes the bur or wire edge produced by a grinding wheel. It also keeps the edge finely tuned, saving you from going back to the wheel. I call this process finish-sharpening.

- Stones give you a longer-lasting edge. While you can achieve a very sharp edge with motorized grinding and buffing wheels, scratches are usually left on the edge, which result in jagged points that make the edge brittle. Medium and fine bench stones leave smaller scratches and consequently smaller points. The smaller these points are, the longer they tend to last before breaking or wearing off.

- If you have only a few tools, it's probably not economical to purchase a grinder or power sharpening unit. An assortment of stones will suffice if your tools require only a touch up.

- If you work with bench stones, you don't have to contend with the irritating sound and volume of most motorized sharpening systems.

- When taking needed breaks during the carving process, touching up edges on a bench stone should be done and can actually be relaxing.

In was in the late-1800s that harder materials for rotating stones were sought after. Materials called silicon carbide and aluminum oxide were developed. Cost efficient and able to put an edge on steel, these materials made their way into bench stones. In recent years, diamond and man-made ceramic stones have put their mark on tool sharpening.

Are Bench Stones for You?

Power sharpening is becoming more popular today, with horizontal and vertical grinding wheels proliferating, and I own both kinds. Needless to say, if your tool has a chipped edge or is very dull, it can be foolhardy to attempt to bring the edge back on a bench stone. Moving the tool back and forth on a stationary stone, even one that is coarse, can take an excruciatingly long time. However, some coarse stones described below will restore a dull or damaged bevel if you have the patience.

Shapes

Bench stones are available in a variety of sizes and shapes. Tapered stones have both concave and convex surfaces that are ideal for gouges. The slip stones on the market offer either small convex edges that are excellent for small gouges or tapered edges for V-tools. Some have both profiles. Square stones can be purchased that are suitable for chisels, 90-degree V-tools, and large gouges. Still others are shaped like rods—useful when touching up the inside of a gouge's bevel—and files, which are helpful for knives, axes, adzes, and drawknives.

Storage

Both oil and Arkansas bench stones usually come in wooden boxes. It's a good idea to keep them enclosed in these containers, especially if wood dust is a problem in your shop or work area. Wood particles will clog the surface of the stone and reduce the sharpening efficiency. If a box is not available or if you want to store those specialty stones such as slip stones and tapered stones, try a plastic storage container. It is readily available at home centers and won't damage the stones.

It is preferable to store a water stone in water if you like to start sharpening immediately. Otherwise, the stone will have to be immersed for a while before use. In most cases, though, water stones can be allowed to dry out without problems. However, they must never be allowed to freeze—any water in them will cause cracks and breaks.

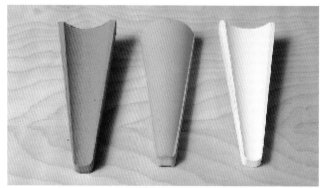

Tapered slip stones, because of their shape, are excellent for gouges. They remove the bur or wire edge created by coarse sharpening or power grinding and they put a fine edge on a bevel. Pictured are Japanese tapered stones.

Lubrication

Let me offer a few words about lubrication. Old-fashioned grinding wheels typically moved through a trough of water. Many of the wheels today have water-drip systems or water reservoirs. The water is necessary to keep the steel from heating up and losing its temper, which is the process of hardening steel through heating and cooling. For bench stones, lubrication is necessary because it contributes to the sharpening process. First, the lubricant helps prevent the stone from clogging up with the minute particles of tool steel left on the surface (called glazing). And second, the sludge created when the stone's loosened grit mixes with the lubricant (called slurry) actually contributes to the sharpening process. Be advised that the coarser the stone, the more lubrication is needed—the absorption into the stone is greater.

Many carvers have the mistaken notion that only oil can be applied to a bench stone. While it's true that oil cannot be used with silicon carbide and some other stones, I prefer water for all other bench stones. Oil is much more difficult to clean up than water. If it gets on my hands and then on a carving, a stain is produced that can adversely affect the finish. Water, on the other hand, dries quickly and will not leave a mess on the wood, clothing, or bench top.

Types of Bench Stones

To help you understand the degree to which a stone sharpens, you need to understand bonding. A hard bond results in a stone that wears slowly. Typical stones with hard bonds go by the names of Arkansas, oil, and ceramic, the last having the hardest bond. In all of these stones, the abrasive grit is surrounded by and almost immovably imbedded in the structure of the stone. The nature of the bond, however, creates a comparatively slow cutting action. Instead of the top layer washing away and exposing new grit, it stays in place—what results is a glaze. When enough steel particles are rubbed off the tool and imbedded in the pores of the bond, the result is a dull or glazed surface. The problem of glazing in a flat stone can be remedied by regularly lapping (rubbing) it on a flat diamond stone or 150 to 220-grit wet-and-dry sandpaper backed by a machined metal surface or glass. Lapping in a circular motion removes the unwanted steel. Only a small amount of lapping is required to remove the glaze. You will notice immediately how the performance of the stone is improved.

Oil Stones

An old standby and still a good choice is the oil stone, which comes in a variety of shapes to accommodate almost every carving tool from a knife to a gouge. Described as a synthetic stone, the abrasive consists of aluminum oxide or silicon carbide. The abrasive is set in a clay-like material to create a hard bond. For a lubricant, a medium-weight oil or kerosene is recommended. The aluminum oxide oil stones are available in finer grits than the silicon carbide stones, but they are not available in very fine grits. It is important when using an oil stone to wipe it with a clean, dry cloth to remove the tiny steel particles that clog the surface. When the particles do build up in the pores, then you will have to turn to a diamond stone or sandpaper. If the stone is tapered, round or V-shaped, gentle sanding with wet-and-dry paper removes the particles of steel.

Stones glaze because the pores get filled with metal particles from tools. Since the glaze reduces the stone's ability to sharpen, lapping is the best remedy. Here an Arkansas stone is lapped with a diamond stone. After lapping in a circular motion for five to ten seconds, the glazing is gone.

Arkansas Stones

Naturally formed from a mineral called novaculite, the Arkansas stone was once considered to be the best sharpening stone by many woodworkers and woodcarvers. I use past tense because, in general, the quality of novaculite deposits has declined while quality synthetic stones have become available. However, Arkansas stones are still good choices. When you do come across Arkansas stones, which are available as bench and slip stones, you will discover they are graded coarse to fine in the following order: Washita, which is fairly coarse but fast cutting; soft; hard; black hard; and translucent. Either water or oil must be used as a lubricant when sharpening on these stones to prevent glazing. And, like oil stones, they need to be wiped clean after use.

Ceramic Stones

Using aluminum oxide as the abrasive, the man-made ceramic stone is set in an extremely hard bond. The advantage is it sharpens quickly and keeps its shape for a long time. The disadvantage is worn and rounded abrasive grits stay in place. The result is a reduction in sharpening speed. To deal with the problem, I lap my flat ceramic stones often with a diamond stone.

Ceramic stones are available in only three grits: medium, fine, and ultra-fine. While sharpening can be accomplished without a lubricant—some catalogs suggest it is not needed for this stone—I use water. I have found that without the lubricant, the stone quickly glazes.

Japanese Water Stones

A decided advantage to water stones is their soft, porous resin bond. When sharpening, the top layer of abrasive grit is slowly but constantly washed away to expose new, sharp abrasives. This action is what accounts for the faster sharpening ability of these stones. However, they will wear more quickly than their harder counterparts described above. I recommend these stones be lapped regularly to keep them flat. A diamond bench stone or wet-and-dry sandpaper backed by a metal plate or glass is needed.

The most commonly used abrasive in the Japanese water stones is aluminum oxide. They possess the greatest grit range of any stone: from about 100 to 8,000. The 6,000- and 8,000-grit stones cut and polish finer than any other type of stone. If you want to keep a flat and unmarked surface, don't let a tool corner dig into the stone.

Diamond Stone

Diamonds are the hardest material used for sharpening devices and will put an edge on just about anything, including carbide. But their real asset is how fast they sharpen.

Diamond stones consist of either monocrystalline or polycrystalline diamonds. The difference for a carver, aside from the fact that the monocrystalline stone is more expensive, is the polycrystalline grit fractures and breaks down over time, leaving a finer and finer grit size. Consequently, it takes longer to sharpen a tool.

The typical grit range for diamond stones is 220 to 1,200. Because the coarser stones cut so aggressively, they produce grooves in the cutting edge. A fine stone such as a black hard Arkansas is recommended for a second round of sharpening. If you do use diamond stones without a lubricant, metal particles will eventually clog them.

Flexible Stones

3M Corporation manufactures diamond stones. Rather than using a metal plate, the company produces a finely graded diamond grit on a piece of flat plastic. Even more novel are the flexible adhesive strips that can be cut to any size or shape you desire. This feature allows you to make your own slip stones, cone or rod-shaped sharpening devices, or files. Even a hook knife will no longer pose a sharpening problem.

Recommendations

Every carver should have at least one full-size bench stone measuring 8 inches long and at least 2 inches wide. A wide stone will provide a surface big enough for a large chisel or gouge if you own one or might purchase one in the future. I do recommend, in addition to the flat stone, a fine-grit slip stone and a leather strop to remove even the smallest bur left after sharpening with a bench stone.

Hand Sharpening
Made Simple

By John Mignone and Roger Schroeder

Unfortunately, there is no "right" method to sharpen—only a correct outcome. You want a tool that can shave a thin slice off end grain as easily as cutting with the grain. Sharpening by hand can be done almost as quickly as by machine and with results just as good. But before you go out and buy the sharpening accessories, take a closer look at these three terms: bevel, bur, and polishing.

Getting the Right Bevel

The tool's bevel determines whether or not it will carve. Carvers all have their own favorite bevel angle, but you generally want to increase the angle as you increase the hardness of the wood. One rule of thumb is to use a shallow angle (15° to 20°) for easily carved woods, such as pine and basswood, and steeper angles (25° to 35°) for harder woods, such as oak and walnut.

Why do you need different bevels for different woods? The shallower the bevel, the easier the tool slides through the wood. But shallower bevels also give you a weaker edge. You can use a shallow bevel for hardwoods, but the sharp edge won't last as long—so you'll need to sharpen more often. You can also use a steeper bevel for softwoods, but it will be harder to push the tool through the wood. When using harder woods, carvers usually use mallets and chisels, so a steeper bevel works fine.

Although there are exceptions, generally a flat bevel is desirable. A rounded bevel makes the tool roll out of the cut prematurely. A hollow ground bevel makes the cutting edge brittle and subject to quick dulling.

Double Bevel

Another sharpening problem is the double or blunt bevel—an extra bevel, or what might appear as a blunt edge, exists on the end of the tool. Sometimes the manufacturer may be the culprit, but it may be the result of your own sharpening. Double bevels result from sharpening at inconsistent angles and can make it difficult for the tool to enter and leave the wood smoothly—the tool will feel sharp but won't cut efficiently.

Holding a Constant Bevel

There are jigs and holders available for most sharpening needs, but it's sometimes just as easy to learn to sharpen by hand. When shaping a bevel, the most important thing is to keep your angle constant—otherwise you will get a double bevel.

Position the sandpaper and glass or sharpening stone so its length is perpendicular to the front of your body. That way you can eyeball the angle of the tool to the paper or stone and maintain a constant angle throughout the sharpening process. For tools like gouges and chisels with short bevels, place a visible angle guide at the end of the glass to help you keep the angle constant. Check out the chart for the suggested motions to sharpen each tool.

Sharpening at a Glance

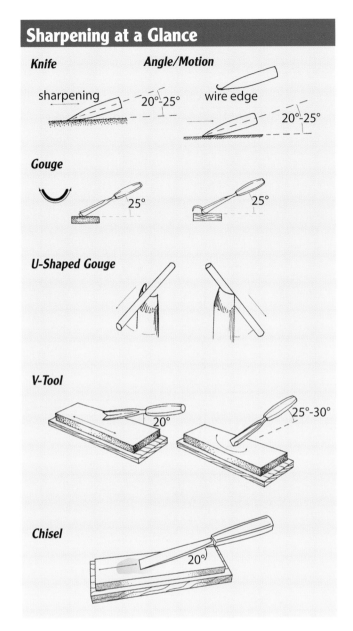

When sharpening, keeping the elbow of the handle-gripping hand close to the body reduces the tendency for the cutting edge to move up and down.

Use a side-to-side motion with the gouges and V-tools. If you attempt to sharpen with the direction of the bevel, even the finest grit will create a slightly scalloped edge, which will give you a jagged cut.

Fresh, bright metal is exposed on the bevel through the sharpening process. If you have trouble seeing your progress, coat the edge with black marker. After the first few strokes, make sure the ink is being worn away evenly. The easiest way to maintain the same bevel is to place the top of the bevel down first and slowly rotate it until the edge rests on the stone.

Sandpaper vs Stones

There are two main ways to shape a bevel—sandpaper and coarse sharpening stones.

Sandpaper

Sandpaper often offers the fastest way to shape a bevel because it is available in very coarse grits. For sharpening, the best choice is silicon carbide sandpaper, commonly referred to as wet-and-dry sandpaper. As the hardest grit, silicon carbide will cut faster and shorten the time spent on the cutting edge. It is also preferred because the paper can be kept wet to aid the sharpening process.

For silicon carbide paper to work efficiently, it needs to be backed with an absolutely flat surface. Your best bet is a ¼"-thick piece of glass measuring approximately 6" wide by 12" long. If the glass slips when you are sharpening, add a piece of non-skid carpet padding to the back of the glass. To hold the paper in place, soak it in water until it is thoroughly wet and smooth it out on the glass, making sure to squeeze out air bubbles. Once the sandpaper is in place, you are ready to sharpen. Make sure it stays wet throughout the sharpening process. Start with coarse sandpaper and use progressively finer grits to remove the scratches left by the previous paper.

Sharpening Stones

A sharpening stone works the same way. The grit in the stone wears away the metal of the blade as it passes over the surface. It doesn't matter if you use diamond stones, oil stones, or water stones. Use a coarse stone until the bevel is shaped and work your way through the finer grits.

Oil stone manufacturers recommend you apply a light oil before sharpening to float the metal particles away. There are commercially available sharpening oils, but carvers I know use everything from kerosene to mineral oil to light-weight motor oil. Some carvers use the stones dry and scrub them off with soap and water regularly—but this isn't recommended by the manufacturers.

Coarse water stones are usually soaked in water, but finer grits just require a spray of water before sharpening. Ceramic stones and diamond stones do not require any lubrication—just a regular cleaning with soap and water.

It is possible to wear a groove into an oil stone or a water stone. Regular re-shaping on a flattening plate or using glass-backed sandpaper is required.

The Bur

The goal of sharpening is to achieve a bur or wire edge. As you sharpen, the metal on the end of the cutting edge becomes very thin and usually rolls over. This is the best indicator that you are very close to having a sharp edge. Continue sharpening until this extra metal is present across the entire cutting edge.

Despite the need to create a bur, it has to be removed; if it isn't, the tool may not cut at all. There is more than one way to remove the bur. Working through finer grits of sandpaper should take it off, especially if you finish sharpening with 1,200-grit sandpaper. Fine sharpening stones, such as a hard black Arkansas stone or the finest-grit water stones will also remove the wire-edge.

Stropping

To make sure the bur is gone and to put a polished edge on your tool, stropping is the last step. Stropping removes the bur and polishes the edge. A polished edge glides through the wood easier. Unless you nick your blade, you can usually just strop a tool rather than re-sharpen it totally.

Choosing a Stone

We offer two tips when purchasing sharpening stones:

1. Choose a stone that does not require oil as a lubricant. It is not only difficult to clean up when it escapes from the surface of the stone, but it can also put an unwanted stain on your project, not to mention the mess on your hands and clothes. Most stones, with oilstones being the exception, work very well with water as the lubricant.

2. It's a good idea to own both a medium and a fine stone to cover a range of sharpening needs. Combination stones are available.

A selection of sharpening stones. From left to right: Hard Arkansas, ceramic, diamond, and Japanese water stone.

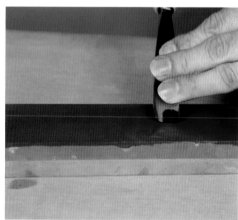

A combination stone is a good choice for fine-tuning a cutting edge and removing a bur before stropping.

To achieve a polished and de-burred edge, strop on a piece of leather coated with an abrasive. Always pull the tool away from the cutting edge.

If sharpening and stropping do not remove the bur, polish it away with a dowel covered with leather, sandpaper, or even stropping compound, as shown here.

All you need to achieve a polished edge is a strop and abrasives or stropping compounds. A carver's strop consists of a piece of hard leather glued to a piece of wood. Two popular abrasives are aluminum oxide and chromium oxide, available in powder, paste, or stick form. Most carving supply companies stock a variety of abrasives and stropping compounds. Note: chromium is a heavy metal and is toxic in high concentrations—avoid contact as much as you can.

To start stropping, apply a small amount of abrasive compound to the strop. To strop gouges, chisels, and V-tools, hold the tool at a constant angle, apply pressure, and pull the tool across the leather. The bevel is held at a constant angle, pressure is applied, and the tool is pulled across the leather away from the cutting edge.

When stropping a knife, lay the blade flat on the leather and pull it with the cutting edge trailing. Resist the temptation to turn the blade up at the end of the stroke. That extra motion will round the bevel, which you want to avoid.

If you push any of the tools or strop them from side to side, you are liable to cut the leather. Stropping is rarely as rigorous as sharpening, but the strokes should be long and firm.

If you see tracks in the stropping compound, the tool probably has a bur. In that case, continue stropping until it disappears. If the bur is still present, return to the finer-grit sandpapers.

Every carver has a different opinion about how often tools should be stropped, but most agree they should be stropped at the beginning of each day of carving. This removes any moisture that may have collected while they were stored.

Removing the Whole Wire-Edge

It is important to remember there are two sides to every cutting edge. And when sharpening, the wire-edge tends to bend over. With straight and skew chisels and carving knives, it's easy to alternate sides to strop off the bur, but gouges and V-tools call for different techniques.

For gouges, bend a piece of leather and push it out of the channel to avoid cutting the material. For a more permanent strop, glue a piece of leather to a dowel. If this proves too troublesome, wrap a dowel that fits inside the channel with a piece of very fine sandpaper. If the paper has a tendency to tear, charge, or rub, the dowel with stropping compound. A charged piece of wood is particularly effective with micro tools.

A traditional way to remove the bur from inside a gouge is to use a slip stone. Slip stones, specially designed for de-burring an inside edge, come in a variety of shapes and are available in many carving catalogs.

For a V-tool, try a charged leather shoelace to remove the bur. A good investment is a knife-edge slip stone, ideal for getting inside V-tools. However, you usually need to sharpen the knife-edge with a piece of sandpaper or a stone—otherwise the slip stone will wear an unwanted groove in the channel of the V-tool.

The Learning Curve

Like any technique, practice may not make perfect, but you'll invariably get better. Work to maintain a consistent bevel angle and avoid shortcuts as you go through the steps to sharpen and to remove the unwanted bur. You may get frustrated that it takes a while to bring a dull edge back to life, but the payback of making polished cuts in the latest project is hard to beat.

Tuning
Up Your
Carving Knife

By Joel Hull

Photography by Roger Schroeder

As a caricature carver, I rely on carving knives to take off wood and refine details. But no matter how much I pay for a knife, there are often problems that have to be corrected even before I make the first cut with a new purchase. While that may discourage some readers, the good news is that in 15 minutes or less, with a minimum outlay of money, a knife can be tuned up and made to cut like a samurai's sword.

Beware of Bevels

In order for a carving tool to perform its function, it must have a bevel—two, in the case of a carving knife. In effect, the bevel forms a wedge that slices and separates the fibers of the wood. For the carving knife, the bevels should be flat on both sides until they taper to the cutting edge. Unfortunately, a knife can come from the manufacturer with any number of issues: a rounded, or convex, bevel; a hollow, or concave, bevel; or a secondary bevel at the cutting edge. And even if these problems are not present with a new knife, an inexperienced carver will likely misshape the tool at some point.

Hollow Bevels

Hollow bevels are most often the result of power grinding. As the tool is pressed into a turning wheel, it takes on the mirror image of the round shape. The downside to a hollow bevel is double-edged: first, it ultimately weakens the cutting edge; second, it does not provide enough support for the cutting edge as it severs wood fibers.

Rounded Bevels

Rounded bevels are troublesome because they require more pressure be put on the blade as it is pushed through the wood. Also, the rounded steel tends to push the edge away from the surface of the wood. Rounded bevels usually result from rocking the blade on a sharpening stone instead of keeping it flat. To better understand how frustrating such a bevel can be, visualize the curved rocker on a rocking chair and how difficult it is for the end to dig into the carpet.

Secondary Bevels

The most common problem I find with carving knives, whether from a manufacturer or from students having difficulty with sharpening them, is the secondary bevel. Sharpening only the edge of the knife causes what some carvers call a double bevel. In effect, a small cutting wedge is formed that makes it more difficult to slice wood fibers.

Honing In On the Problem

When one of these bevel-related issues—or all three—arises with your carving knife, a tune up is in order. I recommend using a sharpening stone. However, I strongly discourage relying on a power sharpening system. In many cases, it was the rotary grinder that created these ineffective bevels. And even if you have a holding fixture and a very large wheel that compensates for incorrect bevels, there is still the risk of overheating the steel. If the temper is lost, be prepared to discard your knife, because it will no longer hold an edge.

Sharpening Stones

Many stationary sharpening stones are available to carvers. They can be made from natural material, aluminum oxide, ceramic, or diamond. My choice for tuning up a knife blade is a polycrystalline diamond honing stone. When the tips of the diamond particles are slowly worn down, new cutting edges are created. No water or oil lubricant is needed, and the surface is less susceptible to a build-up of steel grit from the carving tool. Produced in ¼" and ⅜"-thick plates, these honing stones range in size from 1" by 3" to 3" by 8", and are available in grits as coarse as 270 and as fine as 1,200. The stone I find most useful for tuning up a knife is 600 grit and measures ¼" thick.

Applying the Elbow Grease

Removing any or all of those inappropriate bevels is simple: Roll up your sleeves, lay the stone on a flat surface, take the knife in the other hand, and start stroking or lapping the steel across the stone. A back-and-forth motion will do. Begin with 15 to 20 strokes on one side, turn it over, and do the same on the other side. The technique's success lies in keeping the blade flat on the stone. If you don't, you may find a rounded or secondary bevel that was not there in the first place.

By making a close inspection of the blade, you will see whether the hollow, rounded, or secondary bevel has been removed. If not, go back to the stone and continue lapping, making sure you perform the same number of strokes on each side of the blade.

De-Burring the Wire Edge

When tuning up a bevel on a sharpening stone, steel gets pushed up from the cutting edge without separating from the blade. The result is a wire edge, or bur. If the wire edge is not removed, you cannot cut with the knife.

A simple technique for getting rid of the unwanted edge is to push or pull the blade through a piece of scrap wood. However, I prefer a monocrystalline diamond honing stone. Fine diamond particles are permanently fixed to a flat plastic base. These honing stones should be used with a water lubricant. They measure 2" by 6" and are available in 220, 325, 600 and 1,200 grit. I find 1,200-grit stone is best suited for removing a wire edge.

How many laps are required to remove the wire edge depends on the steel in the blade. But lapping must be done while holding the steel flat on the stone until the wire edge literally falls off. Rocking or rolling the blade will likely recreate bevels you have just removed.

Rounding the Square Edge

There is still another problem associated with carving knives. The square back edge, which looks like it belongs there, actually needs to be rounded. By removing the corners, you improve the knife's ability to "roll" out of a cut. Think of moving a heavy crate by rotating it from one flat side to another. How much easier would it be to move the box if the corners were rounded even slightly? The same physics applies to carving knives.

To round over the corners, I use the polycrystalline diamond plate. In this case, rolling the corners on the plate is not an incorrect technique. If you encounter trouble rounding the corners, try a very fine file.

Polishing

The tune up is not complete until the blade has been polished. Although having a shiny blade looks impressive, the polishing also improves the blade's cutting ability. First, polishing reduces friction resulting from a surface that has honing scratches, no matter how fine they may be. Second, it removes any traces of a wire edge that was not taken away by the very fine diamond stone.

Polishing requires both a leather stropping board and stropping compound. Strops can be purchased from many mail-order retailers, or you can make your own. Make sure the leather is thicker than a dime but thinner than a nickel and glue it to a board—I suggest plywood, which won't expand and contract with seasonal changes—rough side up. A leather piece measuring 2" by 8" handles most knives. Scrape some stropping compound on the rough leather and push it around with a finger until the leather is covered. Lay the blade flat against the leather and press it down firmly. Move the blade along the length of the stropping board with the back edge away from you. Stop, turn the blade over, and pull it forward with the back edge facing you. Make sure not to roll the knife on its cutting edge. If you do, rounding will result, and you will have to start the tune up over.

Removing Nicks

Occasionally, even the most careful carvers put a nick into a blade. Bumping the blade on another piece of steel, dropping the tool, or carving a very hard knot is usually the culprit. While the knife will still perform with a nick, it will leave the inverse impression of a scratch with every cut.

To remove the nick, you need, pardon the pun, to start from scratch. Begin with the polycrystalline diamond stone. After honing, de-burr the wire edge. When that falls off, polish the blade with leather and stropping compound. When your knife leaves a perfectly smooth surface, the nick is gone.

Is It Sharp?

You have labored to remove problems with your carving knife. But will it cut without fighting or tearing the grain? The ultimate test is how well the knife carves. Remove some wood on the edge of a block and run your finger along the newly expose surface. It should feel smooth, with no scratches. If it's rough to the touch, you may have to go back at least one step in the process. However, if you follow the steps I have outlined, your knife will most likely have gone from being a Pinto to a Porsche.

TUNE UP YOUR KNIFE

1

Remove unwanted bevels on a carving knife. Use a polycrystalline diamond honing stone. Holding the knife flat on the stone, make 15 to 20 strokes on each side.

2

Determine if the bevels have been removed. If not, go back to the stone and stroke again. This knife has both a hollow and secondary bevel.

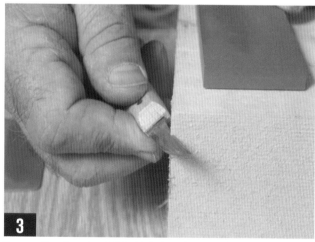

3

Remove the wire edge. Pull the blade through a piece of scrap wood.

4

Another method that takes away a wire edge is to stroke the blade on a ceramic stone or a very fine monocrystalline diamond honing stone.

5

Round the back edge. The square edge on the back of a knife blade makes it difficult to roll the tool out of a concave cut. To round the edge, use the monocrystalline stone. The technique is to roll the edge on the stone.

6

Apply compound. After grating or scraping off pieces of compound with a discarded knife, rub them around on the leather with your finger, covering the entire surface.

7

Strop the knife. Push it along the leather with the back edge facing away from you.

8

Continue to strop. Turn the knife over, making sure that the cutting edge does not touch the leather, and bring the blade back toward you.

9

Test blade sharpness. If the surface exposed by the cuts is smooth and scratch-free, your tune up has been successful.

Sharpening a V-tool

By Charles Berold

Many carvers find sharpening V-tools a challenge. Most traditional methods focus on treating each side of the V as a straight chisel, but there are several steps leading up to the actual sharpening that make it easier to get a sharp edge.

Square up the end. Hold the tool vertically against a 150-grit diamond stone. Move the tool up and down and from side to side until you see little flat areas where the sharp edges should be. You only want to remove the old cutting edge and return the tool to square. If not square, the tool will be difficult to sharpen. Mark the flat areas with a permanent marker (optional).

Shape the side bevels. Hold the tool on one side at a 15° angle. Support it with your index finger and apply pressure in different areas to direct removal of the metal. Maintain the angle and move the tool up and down and side to side. Switch sides often. Use a grinder or sandpaper to bevel the back edge of the diamond stone and use the stone to shape the inside of the tool.

Clean up the edge. Work your way up through 250-grit, 400-grit, 600-grit, and 1,200-grit diamond stones. As you sharpen, steel dust and slivers will obscure the edge. Force the tool into the endgrain of a piece of scrap wood to remove the dust. Work in stages. Remove a little metal, check the edge under a magnifying glass, and repeat until the flat spots disappear.

Remove the hook at the base of the V. This is leftover from the shaping of the sides. Place the point of the V flat on the 1,200-grit stone. Twist your wrist slightly to rock the tool from side to side as you move the tool forward and backward.

Polish the tool. Hold the tool at the same angle used in Step 2 against a leather strop or power strop. Polish the inside of the V lightly with a pointed leather strop. Cut across the end grain of a piece of wood to test the final sharpness of the tool.

Gouge
Sharpening Practice

By Andre Breau

Learning to sharpen gouges can be achieved by following some simple steps. Practice sharpening using a piece of wood molding and sandpaper.

Anatomy of a Sharp Tool

Draw back: Shaping is accomplished by removing the right amount of material so the gouge can penetrate the wood. The first area to shape is the draw back. The further the draw back, the easier the gouge can penetrate the wood, but this results in a thin cutting edge and the gouge might break or chip.

Relief angle: In order to penetrate the wood, the sides— or shoulders—of a gouge are thinned down. These relief angles allow the gouge's shoulders to penetrate for easy chip removal. Relief angles should be long and even for best penetration.

Angle of approach: The draw back determines the angle of approach for the gouge. The angle of approach is the angle at which the gouge starts cutting the wood. The angle of approach varies from one individual to another. Determine the angle of approach you would like and after a few tries, you will find the angle that best suits your needs. A good general angle is 45°. Bent and straight gouges each have different angles of approach.

Cutting edge: The cutting edge is located at the tip of the chisel. To obtain a good cutting edge, good tempered steel is required. Tempered steel requires a minimum of .8% carbon content. Sometimes when the gouges are worn down, a heat treatment is required to give the cutting edge a temper so it will hold a cutting edge. Removing all of the back material will bring the gouges to a good cutting edge.

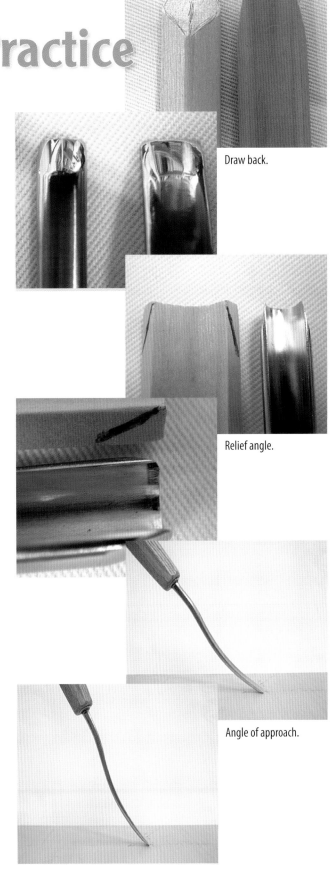

Draw back.

Relief angle.

Angle of approach.

SHARPENING PRACTICE

1

Mark your draw back line approximately ½" from the edge of the wood molding. Marking the line further back on the gouge will give you a thinner bevel and a lower angle of approach. Marking the line closer to the edge will give you a thicker bevel and a higher angle of approach.

2

Sketch in your angle of approach by drawing a line connecting the edge of the gouge with the draw back line. Start shaping the gouge using a back and forth motion on a piece of 120-grit sandpaper.

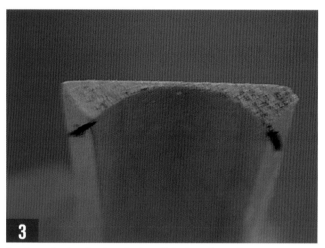

3

Continue shaping the draw back until it is nice and even. Do not try to rotate the gouge to shape the relief angle yet—concentrate on the draw back angle.

4

Shape the relief angles. Use a rotating motion. Remove all the back material until the edge is even and tapered. Continue practicing with cove molding, until it is easy to maintain a steady, even bevel.

5

Remove a small amount of material from the inside of the gouge, using a dowel wrapped in sandpaper or a round stone. This small inner bevel on the gouge will balance the cutting edge, giving it strength and helping it to hold an edge longer.

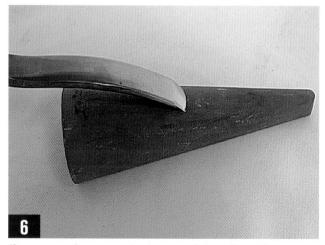

6

Sharpen a regular gouge, using the same techniques. Start with a coarse stone, move to a medium stone, and then use a fine stone. Finish sharpening by adding the inner bevel with sandpaper or a round stone. Polish the edge with a buffing wheel.

Custom
Honing Board

By Lora S. Irish

With just a few minutes of work, you can create this honing board customized to sharpen your specific gouges and V-tools. This honing board is small enough to include with your tool kit, yet large enough to allow extra space for new profiles as your tool collection grows.

The profiles and reverse profiles of this honing board conform to the cutting angle that you use during carving and match your gouge and V-tool exactly.

Materials & Tools

Materials:
- ¾" x 5" x 5" basswood
- Pencil
- Red oxide rouge

Tools:
- Metal ruler or T-square
- Bench knife
- Straight chisel
- Gouges and V-tools to be honed on the board

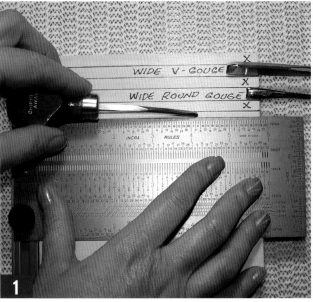

1

Mark the guidelines for your honing board. Place each gouge or V-tool face down upon the wood. Make a pencil mark at the edge of each tool tip. Allow ¼" space between each tool and along the edge of your board. Use a metal ruler or T-square to extend your guidelines.

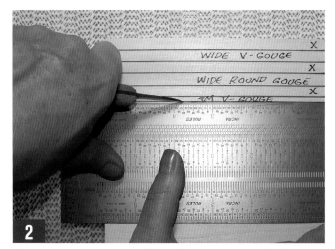

2

Make a stop cut along each guideline. Use a metal ruler and a bench knife. Your board will be divided down the middle. One section hones the bottom of your tools and is used with your tools face up. The second side hones the top side of your tools and is used with the tools face down.

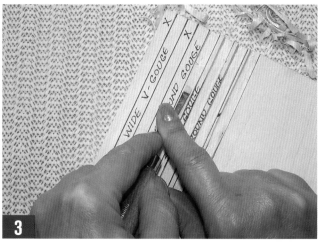

3

Cut the reverse-profile side of your board first. Use a straight chisel to remove the wood in the ¼" spaces and the side margin. Work from the centerline of your board towards one side. This will create a high, flat ridge for each of your gouges.

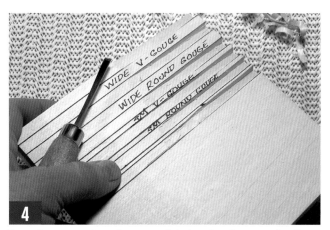

4

Taper these spaces from the center of the board to the outer edge. The depth of the spaces is determined by the sweep of your gouges. With a straight chisel, taper the sides of the high ridges just enough so that your gouge drops over the sides when placed face down on the ridge.

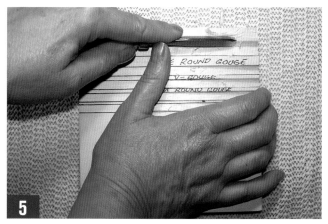

5

Place your gouge face down and begin cutting the ridge. Begin your work near the edge of the board. Move your tool toward the board center. Keep the tool flat to the honing board. When your profile is complete, you should have an inverted V- or U-shape. Cut each reverse profile until the entire tool lies against the wood.

Crumbly Polishing Compound

Most polishing compound is manufactured to charge a spinning buffing wheel and the friction caused by this helps melt the media the compound is suspended in. When using a leather strop for my tools, I find it very difficult to get the polishing compound onto the leather. To charge up my leather stropping board, I melt a stick of polishing compound and add additional beeswax. Once it re-hardens, it is soft enough to rub on the leather with very little effort.

Brian Ehrler
Mansfield, TX

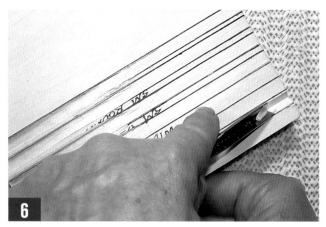

6

Shape the profile side of the honing board. Notice that the spaces between the gouge guidelines have not been cut or removed. Working with your tools face up, cut between the guidelines with each gouge or V-tool. Start your cuts near the edge of the honing board, and with each cut, work back toward the center of your board. Work each profile cut until the entire tool drops into the cut area.

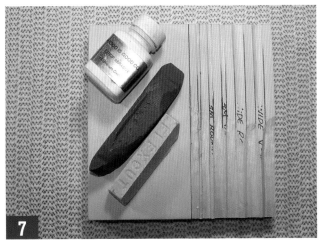

7

Choose your honing compound. The top compound is aluminum oxide, which is available in powder form. The red iron oxide and gold compound are shown in stick form. Red iron oxide compound in stick form contains a wax base that will help the abrasive adhere to your honing board's profiles.

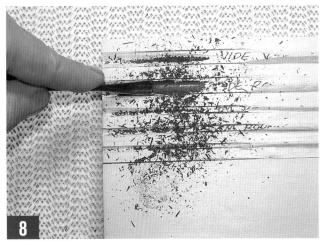

8

Shave a small amount of red iron oxide compound onto your honing board. Use a bench knife. Working the profile side first, push some of the rouge into the profile grooves. Now place your gouge over the abrasive, and pull the tool toward the edge of your board. This will pack the abrasive into the groove area.

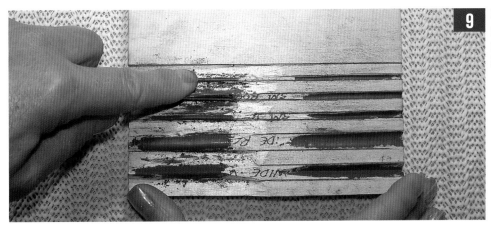

9

Repeat the process for the reverse-profile side. Again, work the rouge onto the profile ridges from the center of the board toward the edge.

Hands-Free Strop

I made this strop to fit the holes in my workbench. If your workbench lacks holes, consider drilling some. It keeps me from having to use two hands to strop, which makes it convenient to reach over and strop my knife more often. It is especially useful when I use both hands on a chisel to maintain an angle. It was well worth the small amount of effort it took to make it.

Dave Dunlap
Kingman, AZ

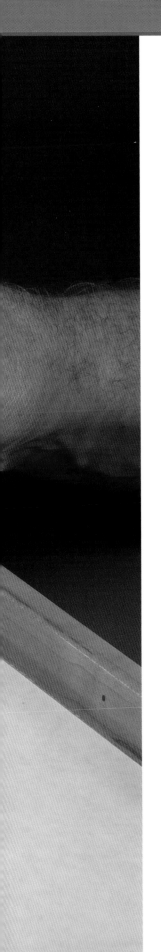

Finishing

This chapter offers helpful tips and explanations to streamline the stages *after* you finish shaping your carving—finishing and display. Always wanted to use an airbrush, but too intimidated? Never able to get the lighting quite right in your photography? Just don't know how to store those scores of paint bottles? The answers can be found here. With these pointers to guide you, you'll finish strong!

One-Stop Finishing Station,
by John Brice, page 116.

One-Stop
Finishing Station

By John Brice

This one-stop finishing station is a great tool you'll use all the time—and you can make it for about $15. The tray uses standard freezer paper (available in grocery stores) as a combination disposable painting surface and palette.

When you've finished your project or need more room for a different color palette, simply pull the paper forward, pull down on the front corner, and tear it off. You can discard the paper, but I find it beneficial to let the paint dry and write my color or mixes right on the freezer paper for future reference.

I've found it pays to buy better-quality freezer paper—the less expensive types tend to bubble when acrylic paints are used. To replace the roll of paper, pull the larger dowel out from one side, replace the roll of paper from the back, and reinsert the dowel.

Building the Tray

I use ½"-thick material for this entire project with birch plywood for the base and solid maple for the side pieces, stop board, and paint tray. Any wood or plywood will work, but I prefer the smoothness of maple and birch grain. A ¾"-diameter dowel is used for the paper roll support, but conduit or PVC pipe works just as well.

Step 1: Cut the pieces to size. I use both a table saw and a scroll saw for the various pieces. On the front edge of the plywood base, cut at a 45° angle (or sharper if your table saw allows). This will allow you to easily cut the freezer paper from the roll.

Step 2: Drill the holes. Use a 1"-diameter bit to drill the holes on the ends of the side pieces (see **Figure 1**) to accept the ¾" diameter x 21" long dowel that holds the freezer paper roll. Use a ¼"-diameter bit to drill five ¼"-diameter holes ¾" deep on the top of each side piece. These holes will hold brushes and other items. Next, using the ⁵⁄₁₆"-diameter bit, drill ¼"-deep holes into the side pieces to accept the two ⁵⁄₁₆"-diameter x 18¾"-long dowels on the base. These dowels will hold down the paper. The ⁵⁄₁₆"-diameter holes are only drilled on the inside of each side piece.

Step 3. Sand the pieces. Using 180- or 220-grit sandpaper, sand each piece. You can hand sand each piece or use a vibrating sander.

Step 4. Nail and glue one side piece to the base. Use a hammer and 4d finishing nails or a brad nailer with 1¼"-long brads to secure the wood every 6". After the glue has set, turn the workpiece over, insert the dowels, and nail and glue the other side piece to the base.

Step 5. Attach the stop board (see Figure 2) **to the paint tray (see** Figure 3). Use nails (or brads) and glue once again. Nail and glue this to the side pieces.

Step 6. Apply a clear spray lacquer of your choice. Follow the instructions on the can and apply two coats of lacquer. Use lacquer, because paint that spills onto the lacquered board can be wiped off.

Re-Purposed Finishing Pad

When painting a carving, put it on a "flower frog" to keep it from sticking to your bench. Flower frogs are lead weights with many sharp tines sticking up, creating essentially a bed of nails. They come in many sizes and shapes. You can usually find them in flea markets and garage sales. If you buy new ones in a craft store, they cost about $4.

Set your carving on one when you paint. Not only do they give you access to all sides, any excess paint drips past the bottom of the carving, and doesn't accumulate, dry, and stick the carving in place. For larger carvings, use more than one frog. They work equally well for spray coating a carving. Spray the bottom first, place it on the frog, and spray the rest of the carving. The carving will not stick to the frog, so finishing is a snap.

Connie Mellott
Brunswick, OH

Crumbly Polishing Compound

Materials:

- ½" x 17½" x 18¼" birch plywood base (one edge cut at a 45° angle)
- 2 each, ½" x 18" x 4½" solid maple (side pieces)
- ½" x 19¾" x 4" solid maple (paint tray)
- ½" x 17½" x 1" solid maple (stop board)
- ¾"-diameter x 21"-long dowel (roll support)
- 2 each, 5⁄16" diameter x 18¾" long dowels (paper hold-downs)
- Sandpaper, 180 or 220 grits
- 18"-wide roll freezer paper (small diameter roll)
- Wood glue
- Lacquer
- 4d finishing nails or 1¼"-long brads

Tools:

- Scroll saw (for curved cuts)
- Table saw (for straight cuts)
- Drill with 1"-, 5⁄16"-, and ¼"-diameter bits
- Hammer
- Vibrating sander (optional)

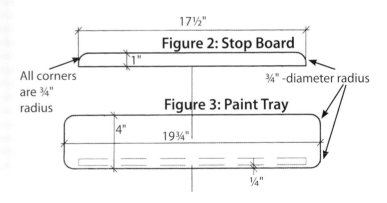

Figure 2: Stop Board

17½"

1"

All corners are ¾" radius

¾"-diameter radius

Figure 3: Paint Tray

4" 19¾"

¼"

Plywod Base

All lumber is ½" thick. The plywood base requires a piece 18¼" by 17½". The righthand 18¼" side should have a 45-degree edge cut.

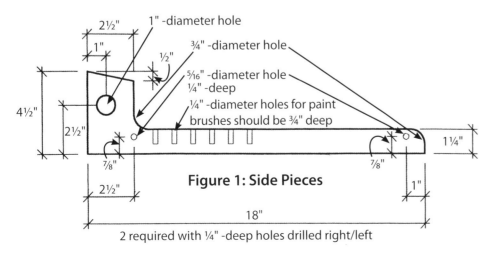

Figure 1: Side Pieces

2½"
1"
½"
1"-diameter hole
¾"-diameter hole
5⁄16"-diameter hole
¼"-deep
¼"-diameter holes for paint brushes should be ¾" deep
4½"
2½"
7⁄8"
2½"
18"
7⁄8"
1"
1¼"

2 required with ¼"-deep holes drilled right/left

Illustrator: Rich Ovans

Paint
Tote Case

By Dick Truesdell

Like many woodcarvers, I have accumulated a sizeable collection of bottles and containers of paint. Storing, organizing, and transporting all those supplies to classes was difficult, so I decided to build this handy case. Done as a weekend project, this paint tote holds as many as 60 bottles and can be built for less than $20 in materials.

Selecting Lumber

I bought my lumber at the local home improvement store instead of at the lumberyard. I was able to purchase it already planed smooth with precise 90° edges. While I could have done the cutting on a table saw and used a jointer for the final clean up, I spent a few dollars more on lumber that did not require heavy power tools. Once I found the boards I liked for the case, I was able to cut the lengths with a circular saw, but even a handsaw will do the job. I chose pine, selecting lengths that were as knot-free as possible. However, other woods such as poplar and maple are ideal, although the case will be heavier and cost slightly more. (See Shopping for Lumber, page 121, for a price comparison and a brief overview of lumber-buying nomenclature.)

The dimensions of the two halves of the case, which are hinged to open and stand upright, depend on the size and the number of the bottles being stored. The paints I prefer come in bottles 1⅜" in diameter. Given that dimension, I was able to use 1x3s to construct the case framework. Other brands offer containers with larger diameters, so 1x4 lumber will probably fit the bill.

Dowel Retainers

To prevent the paint containers from shifting, I designed the case with pairs of ¼"-diameter dowel retainers. To make sure the holes line up on both sides of each half of the case, the sides should be drilled while stacked and clamped together. In fact, it's wise to stack all four sides and drill the holes for the dowels in one operation. To prevent breakout on the lumber, use a brad point drill bit and a scrap board to back up the stack.

I made the pairs of holes 1⅝" apart on center, wide enough to accommodate the typical 1⅜"-diameter paint bottle. Making them slightly closer together will provide a snug fit. Don't worry about not having enough space between the dowels. They are thin enough to have a fair amount of flex.

For easy insertion, drill the holes so they are slightly oversized—¹⁷⁄₆₄" or ⁹⁄₃₂". You can then slide each dowel through from one side of the assembled case and cut off the excess. Hold it in place with glue. If there is too much play in the hole, use epoxy. An alternative method is to drill ⁵⁄₁₆"-diameter holes, insert wood plugs into one side for a more finished look, and glue them in place. Push the dowels through from the opposite side, cutting them to length so dowel plugs can be inserted. Before the glue dries, pull the parallel dowels together with your fingers or turn them if they are slightly bowed to minimize the spacing for a firmer grip on the bottles.

Assembly

The case framework consists of four sides: two tops and two bottoms. The top pieces need to be reduced to 2¼" wide to allow room for the handles. If you don't have a table saw, the lumberyard or home center should be able to rip the boards to size. Assembly of the case is done with rabbet joints, or the pieces of lumber are simply butted together. Use 1½" #6 wood screws to assemble your case. Predrill the holes and glue the joints, making sure the sides are square before the glue sets up.

Place each half of the case on a piece of tempered Masonite and draw the outline. If you use a square corner of the panel as a guide, you are more assured of having the framework squared up. Use glue and 1" wire nails around the edges of the case to hold the Masonite in place. Apply weight to the backs and allow the glue to dry overnight. Then, put a slight bevel on the sharp edges of the Masonite with a block plane, being careful not to catch the nails.

To install the hinges, clamp the two halves together and mark the location for each hinge. A pair 1½" long x 1" wide will suffice for the case. Solid brass adds a nice touch and the hinges cost less than $3. Make stop cuts for the hardware and use a carpenter's chisel to remove only enough wood to recess the thickness of each hinge. Screw the hinges in place and close up the case. Position a chest latch and attach it with screws.

Shop-Made Paint Organizer

I accumulated a large collection of 2oz. bottles of paints and had trouble storing them in a way that I could easily locate the color I needed. While at a large retailer, I found some rectangular baskets designed to stack on top of each other. They measure 7½" x 8½" x 6" tall with 1⅜"-diameter square holes in all four sides. They look like miniature milk crates. Each basket will hold 44 bottles of paint. I purchased a lazy Susan bearings set for $7, so by combining the four baskets with the bearing, I spent approximately $15 and created storage for 176 bottles of paint.

To make the rack, cut a section of ¾"-thick plywood and attach the lazy Susan mechanism to the bottom of it. Then, attach the first basket to the wood by drilling holes through the wood and using wire ties to secure the basket in place. Stack the other baskets, one on top of each other, and secure them all together with wire ties. It sure beats the $29–$49 price tags on the commercially available paint racks. And if I want to collect more paint, I just add a basket.

Thomas Perrin
Alexandria, LA

Getting a Grip

The paint tote case is designed with two handles (see illustration at right). I advise you to cut out a pattern first and see how your hand grips it. Once you find a fit that accommodates your fingers, trace the pattern onto two ¼"-thick pieces of solid lumber, making them slightly longer than the case is wide. You can use plywood, but it tends to splinter and may require considerable sanding. You will also have one side with a better grade of veneer. Sandwich the two handles together and cut them out on a band saw or a scroll saw. Sawing them at the same time is important because they need to match up for a comfortable grip. Lay the closed case on a flat surface and place the handles between the two halves. Mark their locations with a pencil, making sure they are centered. With the halves open, glue and nail each handle in place and cut off the excess on the ends of the handles.

Shelving It

Shelves keep the bottles upright and separated. Plywood or solid lumber will suffice, and the shelves can be dadoed into the sides or attached to shelf supports. Solid aspen, S4S, is available at most home improvement stores, and it is sold in ¼"-thick sizes. I chose plywood for my shelves. If you don't dado the shelves into the sides, support them with scraps of ¼"-thick wood or plywood. Nail both shelves and supports in place with ¾" wire nails. You may want to drill pilot holes into the sides to prevent damaging the case and shelves.

Additions and Options

I found a 1½" diameter x 12" long plastic plumbing waste pipe with a flange on one end makes a great brush holder. Plug the unflanged end with a piece of wood and screw the plug in place to prevent the brushes from sliding out. Use a piece of foam at the other end to hold them. To make a convenient place for the holder when painting, put a small piece of sticky-backed Velcro on one side of the holder and on an outside edge of the case. If you don't have the case completely filled, you may have room to transport the holder inside.

While it's not essential, you can glue 1¼"-square foam strips, used for sealing around an air conditioner, 3" above each shelf to ensure the bottles stay in place when the case is moved or in the event it falls over. I recommend using the foam if you do not have a shelf fully loaded.

The Finishing Touch

Regardless of the wood you choose, a good finish will give this project a professional look and keep the wood clean. Staining is optional, but the case should be coated with a varnish. Medium gloss polyurethane is a good choice. Apply the varnish only to the solid wood or plywood. Masonite becomes dull if varnished, so leave it unfinished. Use painter's tape to mask off the backs before finishing the case.

Materials & Tools

Materials (for a case that holds 60 1⅜"-diameter bottles):

- ⅛" x 24" x 48" Masonite for backs
- Approximately 14' of 1x3 lumber for framework
- Approximately 6' of ¼" x 2½" plywood or solid wood for shelves
- Six 3' lengths of ¼" dowels for retainers
- 1½" long x 1" wide brass hinges
- 2¾" chest latch
- #6 1½" wood screws
- 1" wire nails
- Medium gloss polyurethane

Storing Varnish

After you open a can of varnish for the third or fourth time, the lid gets bent, and air leaks in. The next time you go to use the varnish, it's all set up and dry. To prevent this, pour the varnish into a glass Mason jar and put on the standard two-piece jar lid (the flat cap and the screw ring). If the flat cap gets damaged, throw it away and put on a new one; they're cheap. Store the varnish-filled jar inside a box to protect the varnish from damaging light sources.

Claude Freaner
Lake Ridge, VA

Paint Tote (one half)

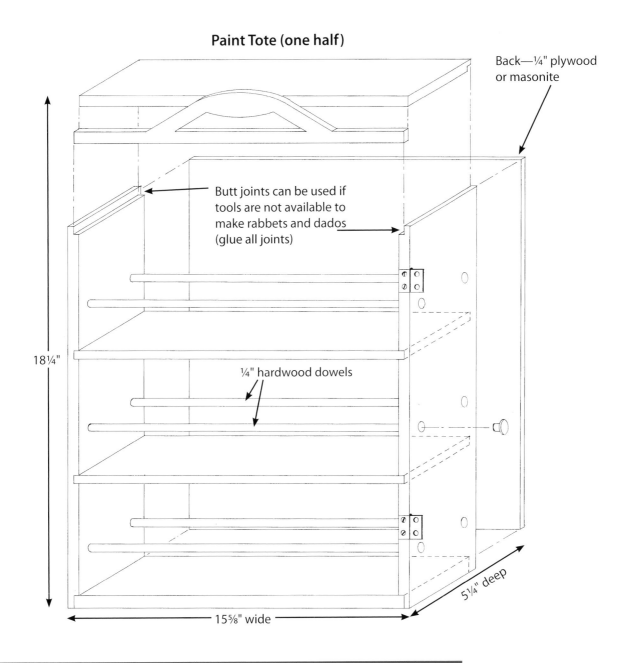

Back—¼" plywood or masonite

Butt joints can be used if tools are not available to make rabbets and dados (glue all joints)

¼" hardwood dowels

18¼"

15⅝" wide

5¼" deep

Shopping for Lumber

To help you make some cost comparisons, I offer prices for wood from a local store. When purchasing lumber, you need to be aware of measuring idiosyncrasies and nomenclature. A 1x3 is actually ¾" x 2½", and a 1x4 is ¾" x 3½". When you see the word "clear," it means the wood is free of knots. S4S stands for wood sanded smooth on all four sides. And knotty pine stands for "a few solid knots."

Wood	Size	Cost
knotty pine	1x3 by 8'	$2.57
knotty pine	1x4 by 8'	$2.95
clear maple	1x3	$1.25 per foot
clear maple	1x4	$1.95 per foot
clear poplar	1x3	$.78 per foot
clear poplar	1x4	$1.05 per foot

Painting
Supplies

By Vicki Rhodes

Everyone knows you need paint and paintbrushes to paint. However, there are a variety of other useful items to make the experience more efficient and enjoyable. The following items are the ones I find most beneficial.

Brush soap. Brushes should be cleaned well with a good-quality soap when you finish painting. While painting, rinse the brushes in water and occasionally dip them into an extender, such as Jo Sonja's Retarder, to keep the paint from drying in the bristles until you have time to clean them.

Containers for water. You'll need two water containers: one to rinse the paint from your brush and the other to pick up water as you paint. Dirty water will change the color of your paint, so keep this container clean. A useful addition to your painting supplies is a brush basin divided into two sections with ridges in the bottom. Gently stroke brushes across the ridges to get all of the paint out.

Containers for mediums such as flow medium and clear glaze medium. You will need at least two small containers to hold mediums. These can be anything from the cap for a bottle to small candle cups or eggcups.

Disposable acrylic palette paper. Paper palettes are available in pads. These are needed for color mixing and dry palette blending. Make sure the paper you select has one slick side. Pads of palette paper listed for use of both acrylic and oils, which do not have the slick side, may absorb the moisture from acrylic paint too quickly.

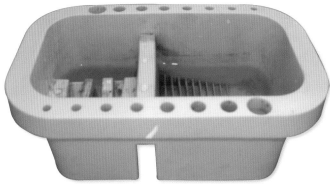
Brush basin.

Soapstone. Soapstone, or plumber's chalk, comes in a stick. It is available at hardware stores in the plumbing supplies. Sharpen the soapstone with a pencil sharpener as needed. This is used to sketch onto the surface because the lines are easily removed.

Towel for work area. An old towel or cloth protects the work surface and provides a cushion for your project.

Distilled water in a squeeze bottle. Use distilled water if storing your palette of colors in a closed container for any length of time. Some tap water contains mold that may grow and contaminate the paint.

Palette knife. A plastic, bent-blade palette knife is great for mixing colors and mediums. They're inexpensive and easy to clean.

Paper towels. Use inexpensive paper towels to set up your wet palette. Thick paper towels may be used for wiping your brush when painting. Fold them into quarters to save space in your work area.

Pencil and pencil sharpener. A #2 HB pencil is the easiest to find. Your pencil may be used for drawing or making notes in your sketchbook. The pencil sharpener will also be used to sharpen soapstone.

Sandpaper. Small pieces of various grits of sandpaper are used both for surface preparation and painting. Medium- or light-colored sandpaper will not lose its color on the background. Fingernail files, which are available in a variety of grades, are excellent for hard to reach places.

Sketchbook or journal. A spiral bound sketchbook or a small journal should be kept for gathering inspiration, color samples, and notes. Glue a Mylar pocket from an office supply store to the back to hold small things.

Wet palette. A wet palette is used for paint storage and may be set up using any shallow container. A wet palette may be as simple as a paper plate or a foam meat tray. An airtight container for food storage will keep paint workable for several days or weeks. Lay a damp paper towel on top of your palette, and apply the paint on top of the paper towel.

Wet palette.

Brush Basics

By Lori Corbett

Brushes that carvers should be familiar with include the following shapes, from left to right: bright, flat, oval wash, round, ultra round, fan, filbert and cat's tongue.

Your finished carving is a thing of beauty, perhaps your finest work so far. All that it needs to elevate it to masterpiece status is paint. You head to the art supply store for paints and brushes where you seem naturally to select quality paints because you know the importance of good colors. Next, you head to the brush department. The paints cost a little more than expected, so you end up scrimping on the brushes. You begin to think one style of brush will substitute for another. A round brush with the beautiful point will not only serve as your detail brush, but also hold enough paint to function as a basecoat and wash brush as well. In fact, if you press hard enough, it spreads open to resemble a fan, which takes care of yet another operation. If that does not suffice, you discover five or six brushes can be purchased for around $15.

Things go downhill when you begin to paint. The basecoat-detail-wash brush you brought home won't hold a point, and hairs stick to the carving. Believing you failed as a painter, you quit in disgust. Whatever made you think you could paint in the first place?

While good-quality paints are important, it is vital that you have the correct brushes for the task at hand. Poor brushes account for a lot of poor results, which are usually blamed on lack of talent. Granted, great results certainly do rely on a great deal of practice. But having a good brush and knowing the effect that brush is likely to produce will allow you to concentrate on technique. There aren't many things in my mind more frustrating than a battle of wills between my brushes and me. The proper brush should become an extension of the painter, not an adversary.

Despite the enormous and intimidating assortment of brush shapes and hairs on the market, I'll focus here on those typically used to paint woodcarvings. As your skills and confidence increase, you will no doubt find yourself experimenting with others. By all means, do just that. With an understanding of these basics, you will have a solid foundation to build on.

Anatomy of a Brush

A brush has two important components (see **Figure 1**). One is the **tuft**, which consists of hair, bristles, or fiber. It is obviously the most important part of the brush. Bristles and hairs are primarily animal in origin; fibers are generally man-made. Tufts can be made from one type of hair, bristle, or fiber or a combination of the three. The materials in the tuft are chosen for their suitability to a particular technique, paint type, and, in the case of some blends, cost.

The other part of the brush is the **ferrule**. It is what holds the tuft together and in turn is fastened to the handle. The ferrule is either seamed or seamless, with the latter offering better quality. A seamless ferrule means solvents or thinners cannot seep in and loosen the ferrule from the handle. The higher-quality brushes usually have brass or copper ferrules and the lesser-quality brushes—called student grade—have aluminum ferrules. These are soft and easily damaged or deformed.

Tuft Materials

There are many different materials used to make tufts. Some of the most common include the following:

Kolinsky tufts are made from the tail hairs of a type of mink called the kolinsky. A native to Siberia, the animal offers hairs that are golden brown in color. Fabricated from the most expensive tuft material, a kolinsky brush is mainly used for watercolor, but it also works well for oils.

As the name implies, a **weasel** brush is made from weasel tail hair. Reddish brown in color, the finest material originates in China. Called a red sable brush, it is medium priced and offers a good alternative to a kolinsky. The weasel brush is marketed for oils and acrylics. A benefit is it does not wear out as fast as a kolinsky.

A **fitch** brush is made from the hair of a ferret-like animal from Europe and Asia known as a polecat. The hairs are light tan to brownish black. A typical fitch brush is great for oil paints.

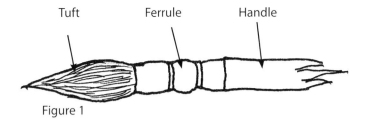

Tuft   Ferrule   Handle

Figure 1

A **squirrel** brush comes from squirrel tail hair. Russian squirrel is best. The hairs are brownish black or bluish black and are used to make fine-quality wash and watercolor brushes. Canadian squirrel hairs are light brown with darker brown tips and are most often made into student-grade brushes. Squirrel brushes are not suitable for applying thick paint, but they are very good for thin paints and inks.

The best **mongoose** brush hair comes from India. The color graduates from dark brown at the tip to cream in the middle to dark at the ferrule. These brushes are marketed under the names royal sable or crown sable. It is a medium-priced brush manufactured for oil painting.

A **sabeline** is an imitation sable brush made from the ear hair of cattle and is dyed to resemble sable. These are student-grade brushes; I do not recommend them. Another brush made from the hair found on the inside of the ears of cattle is the **ox** brush. The color is either light tan or dark brown. This hair is used primarily to make the flat-style brushes.

Made from the body hair of a horse, the **pony** brush is usually dark brown in color. Less expensive than squirrel brushes, pony hair brushes are generally student grade and are not recommended.

A **synthetic** brush consists of man-made polyester or nylon and was developed for acrylic paints. A common name found on these brushes is Taklon. Acrylic painting requires large amounts of water, which swells natural hairs and causes them to break down. Rough-textured surfaces, solvents, and cleaners will also wear natural-hair brushes fairly quickly. Man-made fibers stand up very well to rough surfaces and acrylic paints.

Figure 2a: Bright brush.

Figure 2b: Flat brush.

Brush Shapes

Some of the more common brush shapes and their uses are listed below. Keep in mind that, with a few exceptions, all of these brushes can be made with any of the tuft materials previously discussed.

A **bright** brush has a flat ferrule and a short tuft. The width and length of the tuft are nearly equal, with the end being squared off. Used to make short strokes with thick colors, it does not hold a lot of paint. However, its short length is easy to control. The edge, or chisel end, makes interesting thin strokes (**see Figure 2a**).

A **flat** brush also has a flat ferrule, but the tuft is medium to long in length and is usually twice the length of a bright brush. Also, the end is squared off. This is a fairly maneuverable brush with lots of color capacity. It can be used for long, sweeping strokes, or on the chisel end for relatively thin lines. It also works well to fill in areas with color (**see Figure 2b**).

An **oval wash** brush has a flat ferrule with a rounded tuft, but it does not come to a point. This brush is ideal for laying in large areas of thinned paint. It produces a softer edge, thus creating a smoother transition between different color areas (**see Figure 2c**).

A **round** brush has a round ferrule, and the tuft is formed into a rounded and pointed tip. This is a good all-around brush. I use four different ones for small area washes, filling, thick line work, and spotting (**see Figure 2d**).

Figure 2c: Oval wash brush.

Figure 2d: Round brush.

An **ultra-round** brush has a round ferrule and a sharply pointed tuft. If you are painting a number of fine and repetitive detail lines, this brush is ideal. The barrel holds a lot of paint, which means less reloading and, consequently, your brush stroke rhythm is not broken. This is my favorite brush and the one I use the most (**see Figure 2e**).

A **fan** brush has a flat ferrule and, when the tuft is spread, it resembles a fan. This is a good brush for soft blending of wet colors and for creating soft, wispy effects (**see Figure 2f**).

A **filbert** brush has a flat ferrule and a long, thick, oval-shaped tuft. The brush is useful for blending colors, and the edge can be used to create line work (**see Figure 2g**).

A **cat's tongue** brush resembles a filbert except the flat tuft comes to a point and is traditionally used to paint fine detail. Some carvers use the cat's tongue to create feather edges. This is the one exception to a careful treatment of brushes. In order to use this brush to make feather edges, it must be mistreated a bit. This requires "re-training" the tuft by getting it wet, and then fanning it out by pressing it down on a hard surface until it has a permanent bend and splay. To use this brush, first dampen it, and then load it with a small amount of paint. Touch it to the feather edge and lightly drag it toward you to create a cup-shaped edge. A synthetic tuft is ideal for this technique (**see Figure 2h**).

With just a basic understanding of brush anatomy, tufts, and shapes, the intimidation associated with brush selection should be eliminated and one more obstacle in the path to your masterpiece is removed.

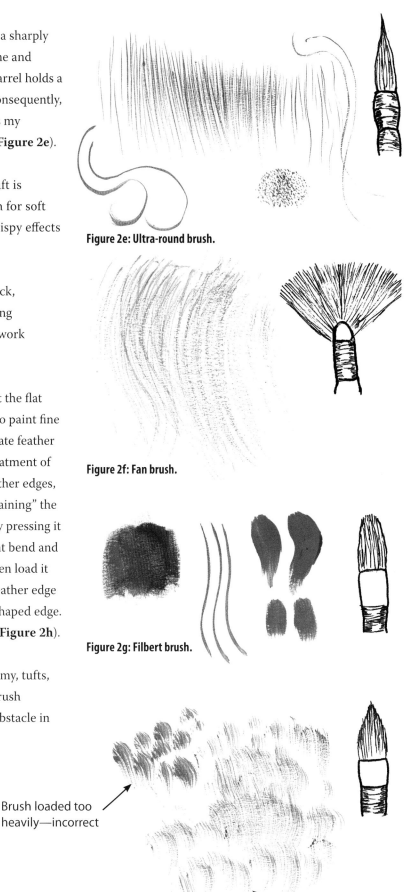

Figure 2e: Ultra-round brush.

Figure 2f: Fan brush.

Figure 2g: Filbert brush.

Brush loaded too heavily—incorrect

Just the end loaded—correct

Figure 2h: Cat's tongue brush

Tips on Buying a Brush

Here are five tips to keep in mind when you go to buy a brush:

- Check the fastening of the ferrule to the handle. If you can move or spin it, the handle will eventually fall out.

- Inspect the ferrule at the tuft end for sharp edges. That sharp edge will cut into the tuft. Occasionally, unfinished ferrules do show up, even on the high-end brushes.

- Do not buy a brush with a vertical gap or split in the tuft. This is a permanent flaw, and the tuft will never retain its proper shape. An example of a split tuft would be a round brush that appears to have two points (**compare Figures 3 and 4**).

- Look for any hard spots in the tuft. This is most often caused by glue seeping into it. When that happens, the glue cannot be removed.

- Check shredding. There are several factors that cause a brush to shed, including misuse. The main reason for shedding is insufficient glue. Another is the tufts are not crimped tightly into the ferrule. The best way to test for this—I anticipate art store owners cringing—is to gently comb the tuft with an ordinary fine-toothed comb. If long hairs are coming out with some regularity, the brush is defective.

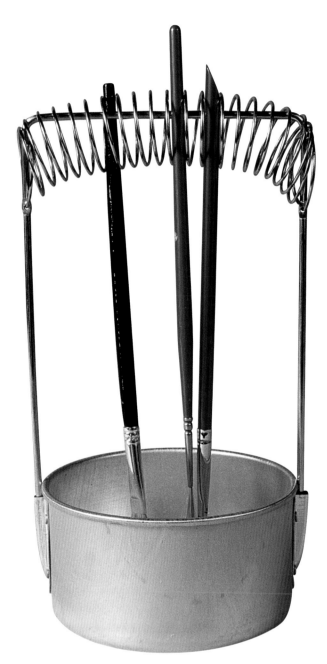

Allowing a brush to sit on the bottom of a water container can ruin the shape of the tuft. A brush holder saves the shape by suspending it over the bottom.

Brush Care

I recommend rinsing a brush often when using acrylic paints. Once the paint dries, it is nearly impossible to clean and restore the brush to anything near its proper state. Also, don't let the brush sit for a long period of time in the water jar with the tuft resting on the bottom. This will permanently bend it and ruin the shape. It takes seconds to rinse and reshape a brush after each use. Or, you can purchase a brush holder. A spring-like device that sits over the top of the water jar, it holds the brush suspended in the water above the bottom.

When painting, do not load a brush to the ferrule with paint. Some paint always seems to be left behind after cleaning. Eventually, it will build up, causing the tufts to spread (see **Figure 5**). When that happens, the brush will permanently lose its original shape. However, don't throw away that ruined brush. It makes a great blending brush, especially for the technique called scrubbing or scumbling. By scrubbing together two or more adjacent color areas that are still damp, a smooth transition is formed between them.

A brush is best cleaned with warm water and a cleaning solution or mild soap. Then, load it with a retarder medium and reshape it before storing. Another trick is to clean the brush, pat it dry, and apply ordinary hair conditioner to it. Then, wipe the brush back and forth on your hand until you can no longer see any excess conditioner. Once it is dry, shape the brush and store it upright.

The cleaning technique is the same for watercolor paints. For oil paints, the technique is the same except a cleaning solvent made for oil colors is required. Once the brush is clean, remove the solvent with warm, soapy water, rinse, and pat the brush dry.

If you insist on using a protective plastic cap on a brush (see **Figure 6**), don't use the one that originally came with it. The cap was intended only as protection during shipping. It is very difficult to replace the cap without catching a stray hair or two (see **Figure 7**). Once the hairs are bent, they stay that way. Instead, use a larger size or, better yet, discard the cap and don't tempt fate.

The best way to store a brush is upright. The less the tuft touches anything, the longer it will last. If the brush is clean but still damp, suspend it with the tuft down until it is dry.

If you live in a small community as I do, you probably order your brushes from catalogs. I buy no less than three of each type. If any are defective, I will most likely have one to use right away. In any case, I like to have extras on hand at all times just in case something bad happens to one of them. Some brushes, like the ultra-round detail brushes, I replace frequently, often after every two or three bird carvings.

A paintbrush is a tool, every bit as important as a quality carving tool. Give yourself a fair chance at painting. Purchase a good quality brush that is the right material and shape for the job. The results will pay off.

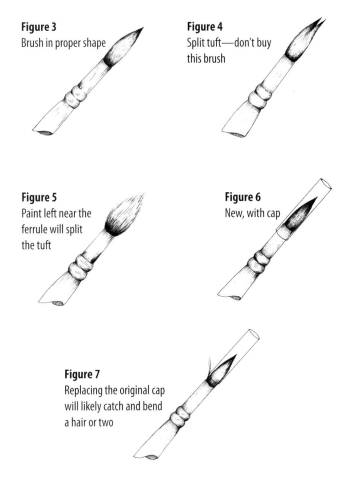

Figure 3
Brush in proper shape

Figure 4
Split tuft—don't buy this brush

Figure 5
Paint left near the ferrule will split the tuft

Figure 6
New, with cap

Figure 7
Replacing the original cap will likely catch and bend a hair or two

Airbrush
Basics

By Jack Kochan

When I give presentations on airbrush use, I tell my audience airbrushing is not the final answer to every finish. Instead, it is a good supplemental tool that can be used on almost every carving project. And since most carvers are not highly skilled with paints, problems of applying a finish can be eased with some basic knowledge of airbrushing equipment and techniques.

An airbrush is an ideal way to enhance many projects.

The Whys of Airbrushing

While I am interested in all styles of carving, I gravitate to wildfowl and to my airbrush, when it's time to paint. I choose this tool because I am not particularly adept at blending with a bristle brush. With even an inexpensive airbrush, I can blend paints like a Dutch master and vary the intensity of a particular color to create highlights and shadows.

An airbrush can, of course, tackle many kinds of projects besides carved birds. If you become skilled with it, you can pinstripe an automobile or paint ceramic ware. Caricature carvers will appreciate the way the airbrush distributes colors. Instead of brushing on an excessive amount of stain, waiting for it to soak in, and then wiping it off, you spray the stain on the project until you obtain the desired effect. Then, you simply stop. Less stain is used, and there is more control over the depth and intensity of color.

I spray acrylics, but carvers who prefer oil paints, enamels, gouaches, watercolors, and varnishes will have no trouble using the airbrush as the application tool. In fact, there is little the airbrush cannot spray, provided the medium is thin enough to pass through a narrow-opening nozzle.

Airbrush Principles

With only a rare exception, almost all airbrushes work on the same principle: A medium, such as paint, mixes with air and comes out of a nozzle. To help you visualize the physics of an airbrush in use, go to the kitchen, find two soda straws, and fill a glass with water. Stand one straw in the glass, position the end of the second straw near the top of the upright straw, and blow through it. A decrease in air pressure is created, and the water rises in the first straw. That is how an airbrush works with, of course, a lot of mechanical refinement.

Much to a first-time airbrusher's sigh of relief, the medium—called paint from this point on—does not shoot out of the nozzle in a fan-shape spray, a phenomenon we experience with a garden hose. Instead, the spray pattern comes to a fine point, then inverts and begins to expand. When you position the nozzle tip very close to an object, the paint can literally leave a pinpoint dot. As you move the nozzle away, the pattern of paint distribution becomes larger. For that, you have an airbrush needle to thank.

Needles and Airbrush Action

The body of a typical airbrush looks like a fountain pen. While a pen has a refill as its main component, the airbrush has a needle. Nothing more than a smooth, rigid, and pointed wire, the needle slides into a small hole in the nozzle. When it is fully inserted, the tolerance between the needle and hole is zero, and the paint will not flow. To make the paint come out, you need to master airbrush action.

On the top of most airbrushes is a small knob. Depress it and a valve is opened that lets air flow into the airbrush. Think of how air is released from a bike tire when the valve pin is pushed in. A single-action airbrush, the simplest variety, does nothing more than this operation, spraying the paint at a preset rate. A double-action airbrush, by comparison, has both a valve release and trigger action. Push down on the knob and then pull it back. The first action controls the airflow while the trigger-release motion governs how much paint flows from its source. Remember the procedure with the following rule: Depress the knob and air comes out; pull it back and the paint comes out.

It is not just the needle and nozzle doing the work of spraying, however. Look at the end of the nozzle, and you will discover small holes around its perimeter. These suck in air and further shape the pattern of the spray.

A beginning airbrusher may find the double action challenging at first. After a week's worth of projects, however, the operation of almost simultaneously pushing and pulling will become second nature. I prefer to depress the knob with the knuckle of my index finger. Other grips will work just as well with practice. On the practical side, a single-action airbrush makes controlling the flow of paint much more difficult. I estimate the more versatile double-action airbrush offers ten times the flow control over its simpler counterpart.

Paint Source

Some airbrushes have a built-in "fluid vanity." This internal source makes it ideal for artists seeking to achieve very precise detail, while only very small amounts of highly thinned paints are needed. But such an airbrush probably won't be practical for finishing woodcarvings. External color cups will either be a top-feed or a bottom-feed setup. The cup of a bottom-feed rotates to one side or the other. In either case, the paint and air are mixed inside the airbrush.

Keep It Moving

A not-so-secret approach to successful airbrushing is keeping the tool in motion. Holding the airbrush in one place builds up paint, resulting in runs and streaks. My advice is to position the airbrush to one side of the project and activate the air and paint. Sometimes, I start to airbrush on a piece of scrap paper and then move on to the project without stopping the flow. In addition, I do not halt the paint flow until I have moved the airbrush away from the project. Stopping the motion before stopping the paint flow leaves a buildup of paint at the end of the stroke that invariably results in runs or streaks.

The issue of distance factors into using an airbrush. How far should you hold the tool from the project? I keep the airbrush in the range of 2" to 6" from my carvings. Precisely what that distance is depends on air and paint flow and the width of spray you want to achieve. Of course, hold the airbrush too far away and nothing will happen because the paint cannot reach the carving.

Airbrush "Accessories"

For an airbrush to work, it needs a source of air. Canned air, both cheap and portable, will last for 15 to 20 minutes of airbrushing time. The drawback is the air pressure is fixed. Consequently, control of the spray is minimized. The solution is an air compressor for virtually unlimited airbrushing time. If it has a pressure regulator, the unit will provide all the control you require. You also need to consider a holding tank, which keeps the compressor from pulsating.

Another essential add-on is an in-line filter to remove moisture that tends to build up during operation. You don't want water droplets dripping onto your project. And to prevent the motor from overheating—resulting in hairline cracks and eventual air leaks—an automatic shut-off valve is necessary.

When you add up the accessories, you can expect to pay around $300 or more. On a positive note, you will not need a particularly large compressor to run an airbrush. Do not bother to look to those home improvement center models that are refrigerator-size. You can fulfill all your airbrushing needs with a much smaller unit. The issue is one of airflow, not horsepower. And a compact unit will give you all the air you need for airbrushing. Some retailers sell an airbrush kit that includes a well-designed compressor, airbrush, and accessories, and others sell the components separately.

I strongly recommend you find a carver who uses an airbrush and give it a try before making the investment. A little investigation will go a long way toward helping you with the decision to buy or not.

Basic Maintenance

The accessories have their own maintenance manuals or sheets, and to cover their contents will take up too much space. Instead, I confine my advice to the airbrush itself, looking first at one of the most common beginner mistakes: not keeping the tool clean. Because the airbrush is such a precision instrument, it should be cleaned with the proper solvent after each use.

For acrylics, I disassemble the airbrush and soak the components in a pan of denatured alcohol. For oil-based paints, I use paint thinner. Lacquer thinner is required for cleaning up lacquer paints; be warned that plastic parts will dissolve in that solvent. When using any of these chemicals, make sure you have adequate ventilation.

I do take some precautionary steps to prevent clogging. After ten minutes of airbrush use, I remove the needle and clean it and the nozzle. In most cases, water is sufficient. After each different color application and when I am finished airbrushing, I put water into the color cup and spray it into a wastebasket with a plastic trash liner. In most cases, this flushing out cleans the airbrush.

A Point of Precaution

The needle deserves some special precautions. If you should drop your airbrush, you risk bending the tip of the needle. Since it is so fine, you may not even notice the problem. The airbrush will still work, but the spray pattern will be askew. More problematic is a bend that leaves a hook on the tip. When that occurs, the hook traps the minute particles and the result is spurts and blotches.

If I think a hook has formed, I drag and rotate the needle across a piece of facial tissue. If it pulls and rips the tissue, it is time to purchase a replacement needle.

The needle is held in place with a locking chuck. After cleaning the airbrush but before storing it, I loosen the needle and back it out of the nozzle a short distance. I also leave the locking chuck loose. Left tightly seated on the needle for too long, the chuck may compress the retaining washer to a point where it no longer grasps the needle firmly.

Airbrush Anatomy

Color cup. A detachable color cup holds diluted paints. On this model, paint is drawn from a bottom-feed cup through suction. The cup can be turned to either side so that it is out of the way of the gripping hand.

Handle. All airbrushes have a plastic or metal handle that covers and protects the internal components.

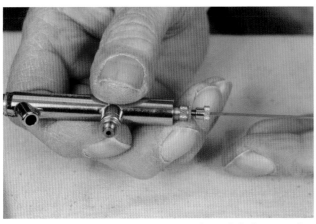

Needle. Inside of the airbrush is a needle. Drawing the needle back increases the flow of paint.

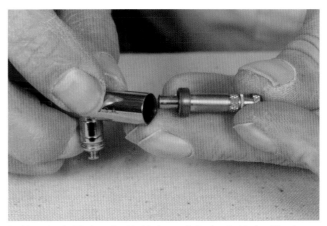

Locking chuck. A locking chuck holds the needle in place inside the airbrush.

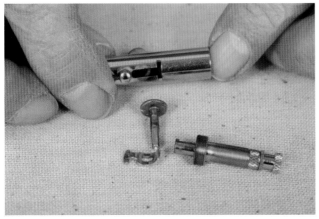

Knob. A knob on top of the airbrush controls the airflow when it is depressed. When it is pulled back, it slides the locking chuck back, which withdraws the needle tip from the nozzle opening. The greater the opening, the greater the amount of paint that comes out.

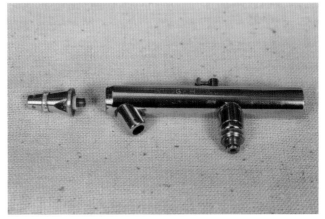

Nozzle. The nozzle, pictured on the left, has small holes that allow more air to mix with the paint and further shape the spray pattern.

11 Tips for Airbrushers

1. For the best results when learning airbrush basics, spray with the nozzle held perpendicular to the surface.

2. When mixing paint with a thinner, aim for the consistency of 1% or 2% milk. Paint that is too thick will not flow through the small opening in the nozzle. If paint falls off a bristle brush after a second or two, you probably have the right mix. If it's too thin, add more pigment; if too thick, mix in more water. Gouache paints are good choices because they have such finely ground pigments. Watercolor paints are also easy to mix.

3. When airbrushing, build up the colors gradually and in layers. Work slowly and let the paint dry. An airbrush actually contributes to the drying process because the airflow removes moisture on the painted surface.

4. Whenever possible, mix a flow medium into your paints. It does what the name suggests—helps the paint flow better.

5. Fill the color cup sparingly. A little paint goes a long way.

6. It is very easy to tip over an airbrush, spilling the contents of the cup or damaging the needle. Most airbrushes come with a hanger than can be attached to the edge of a workbench. If one is not available, purchase a holder.

7. Using acrylic paints may not pose a health problem, but don a paint or dust mask anyway if airbrushing for any length of time. When spraying oil paints or lacquers, ventilation is a must. If you do not have adequate ventilation, consider building a small painting booth out of a cardboard box with a small fan and furnace filter in the rear.

8. Put the protective cap over the nozzle when storing the airbrush.

9. Maintain pressure between 18 and 30 psi (pounds per square inch). More pressure reduces control and poses a safety hazard. A good range is between 25 and 28 psi.

10. Avoid cleaning out the airbrush nozzle with a cotton swab. Even a single fiber of cotton can adversely affect the nozzle opening. Facial tissue and a toothpick make a good alternative to a cotton swab.

11. When it is practical, mask off an area prior to spraying. A piece of index card, plastic wrap, or even a finger will serve. A commercial product called Frisket Film is a low-tack, transparent masking material, compatible with all surfaces. It is easy to peel and leaves no residue. When using a piece of paper as a mask, the closer it sits on the surface, the more pronounced the separation of colors. Move the mask off the surface slightly and the colors blend into each other as you airbrush.

Mix paints in a separate container to the consistency of 1% or 2% milk. If the paint drips off the brush after one or two seconds, it is likely the right mix.

To prevent the paint from spilling, or the needle from getting damaged, put the airbrush on a holder. This accessory holds two airbrushes.

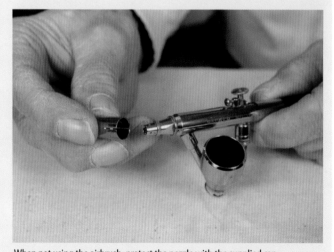

When not using the airbrush, protect the nozzle with the supplied cap.

Paint Mixing
Record Chart

By Lori Corbett

This method of record keeping has evolved over years of keeping color mixing notes on everything from Post-It notes to tongue depressors. I designed this chart for bird carving, but it could be used for other types of artwork.

The chart is divided into two sections. On the top section, note the title of the project and date completed. Then, paint swatches of all the colors used in the blank squares, and in the places underneath, list the brand of paint, the color name, and the Color Index Name, or CIN, for each swatch.

The bottom section is for the mixes used in the projects. The lines through the center of the rectangle serve as both a dividing line for masstone and undertone and an indicator of opacity.

The more opaque a color is, the better it will cover, as shown on the completed chart. Paint a swatch of the undiluted mix in the left half of the rectangle. The more the horizontal line is obscured, the more opaque the color is. This is also the mix in its purest form—its masstone. Dilute the mix with water or glazing medium and paint a swatch in the right half of the rectangle. This indicates the undertone of the mix. This is especially important when you are mixing dark colors because they are more difficult to match than lighter colors. When you mix this color again at a later time, it may appear very similar in masstone, but when you apply the mix as thinned layers (glazes), it may be very different because the proportions may be off. The diluted example helps you match the color more accurately by its undertone. You can see right away if the mix needs to be adjusted. The undertone also lets you see what that mix will look like when diluted for use as a glaze.

Below the rectangle is a space to note the mix number. I correlate this with notes I keep for the steps required to complete the project or area being painted.

Above the rectangle is a space to note where the mix will be used. On the completed chart, you can see the notations are for different areas or color values on a red-tailed hawk feather. For example, on Mix #1, I've noted that it's for the red area on the top surface of the feather.

To the right of the rectangle is an area for listing the individual pigments and the proportions used to make that mix.

Softening Paste Wax

When finishing a carving with a paste wax coating, I like to put a generous dollop of paste wax in a glass bowl and heat it in the microwave for a few seconds until it's nearly liquid. Then, I use a stiff-bristled paintbrush, like a stencil or stippling brush, to coat the carving thoroughly. The stiff bristles let you get down in all the cracks and crannies, and the nearly melted paste wax spreads much easier than it does in its natural condition.

Once the carving is thoroughly covered in wax, use a soft, clean cloth (like a worn out wash cloth or T-shirt) to buff it to a nice luster. Cotton swabs can be used to buff hard-to-reach spots on the carving. This tip was inspired by a conversation with Lora S. Irish on the WCI message board.

Donna Thomas
Nevada, MO

SAMPLE

PAINT MIXING RECORD

SPECIE: _Red-Tailed Hawk Tail Feather_   DATE COMPLETED: _____

Straight tube colors used in mixes. List the brand, color & C.I.N. (Color Index Name) under each swatch. Ex: Brand "X"-Raw Sienna - PBr7

BRAND: Lascaux	Lascaux	Lascaux	Lascaux	Lascaux	Lascaux
COLOR: Oxide Red Deep	Oxide Red Light	Transoxide Red	Transoxide Yellow	Diox. Violet Deep	Oxide Brown Medium
C.I.N. PR 101	PR 101	PR 101	PY 42	PV 23	Pbr 6

BRAND: Golden	Golden	Golden
COLOR: Yellow Ochre	Titanium Buff	Zinc White
C.I.N. PY 43	PW 6	PW 4

COLOR MIXES: Place a sample of the mix in the box & list the colors & quantities used. Note the area where the mix is used above the box (EX: Scapulars, rump primaries, etc.),

The lines through the center of the square serves as both a dividing line for mass tone & undertone, as well as an indicator of opacity. Paint half the square with the full strength color (mass tone) and the other half with a diluted mixture (undertone). The other black line serves to indicate opacity. The more the line is obscured, the more opaque the color.

Red area - Top

# 1	Oxide Red Ligh t= 45%
	Yellow Ochre = 45%
	Diox. Violet Deep = 10%

Dark bands - Top

# 2	Diox. Violet Deep = 40%
	Yellow Ochre = 50%
	Oxide Red Deep = 10%

Mottling @ base -Top & dark bands - Bottom

# 3	Mix #2 = 60%
	Titanium Buff = 40%

Highlights - Top

# 4	Yellow Ochre = 50%
	Titanium Buff = 50%

Shadows - Top

# 5	Mix #1 = 50%
	Oxide Brown Med. = 40%
	Diox. Violet Deep = 10%

Highlights-Bottom

# 6	Mix #4 = 50%
	Titanium Buff = 50%

Main color - Bottom

# 7	Mix #1 = 20%
	Mix #4 = 80%

Shadows-Bottom

# 8	Mix #7 = 80%
	Mix #1 = 20%

Final glaze-Bottom

# 9	Zinc White = 70%
	Transoxide Yellow = 30%

#	

Attach photo or sketch of artwork on reverse side

SHEET ____ of ____

PAINT MIXING RECORD

TITLE:______________________________ **DATE COMPLETED:**____________________

Straight tube colors used in mixes. List the brand, color & C.I.N. (Color Index Name) under each swatch. Ex: Brand "X"-Raw Sienna - PBr7

	☐	☐	☐	☐	☐	☐
BRAND:						
COLOR:						
C.I.N.						
	☐	☐	☐	☐	☐	☐
BRAND:						
COLOR:						
C.I.N.						

COLOR MIXES: Place a sample of the mix in the box & list the colors & quantities used. Note the area where the mix is used above the box (EX: Scapulars, rump primaries, etc.),

The lines through the center of the square serves as both a dividing line for mass tone & undertone, as well as an indicator of opacity. Paint half the square with the full strength color (mass tone) and the other half with a diluted mixture (undertone). The other black line serves to indicate opacity. The more the line is obscured, the more opaque the color.

#_____			#_____		
#_____			#_____		
#_____			#_____		
#_____			#_____		
#_____			#_____		

Attach photo or sketch of artwork on reverse side

SHEET ____of____

WHISPERING EAGLE STUDIO - 530 EAST 5TH NORTH - SAINT ANTHONY, IDAHO 83445 - TEL: 208-624-7717 - EMAIL: lcorbett@cableone.net

In the Best Light:
Photographing
Your Artwork

By Bob Duncan

To get a good photo of a carving, you need to take several things into account. The most important four are image resolution, lighting, focus, and background. We've taken some excellent carvings by experts in their field and photographed them properly—and poorly—to show how a few little tricks can really improve your photographs.

Pixel Conversion

72 dpi			300 dpi		
Image Size	Pixels	File Size	Image Size	Pixels	File Size
4" x 5"	288 x 360	303.8k	4" x 5"	1200 x 1500	5.15M
5" x 7"	360 x 504	531.6k	5" x 7"	1500 x 2100	9.01M
8" x 10"	576 x 720	1.19M	8" x 10"	2400 x 3000	20.6M

Resolution

Resolution is the density of an image. It pertains more to digital photography than to traditional prints or slides.

Resolution is measured in two ways: by the number of pixels, or dots of color, in an image or by the actual size of an image and the number of dots per inch (dpi). For example, a photo downloaded from a standard web page may be 5" x 7" on the screen, but it may only be 72 dpi. In order to print something in a magazine, 300 dpi is needed. A 72 dpi photo looks grainy and out of focus printed at 5" x 7". In order to get the resolution we need, the photo must be shrunk down to the size of a postage stamp.

Most computers show the size of a photo in pixels. For most publications, your photo must be 1200 x 1500 pixels.

For a 5" x 7" photo to be reproduced properly, you need at least a 3-megapixel camera, but a 4- to 5-megapixel camera is preferred. The resolution of camera phones is too low to reproduce.

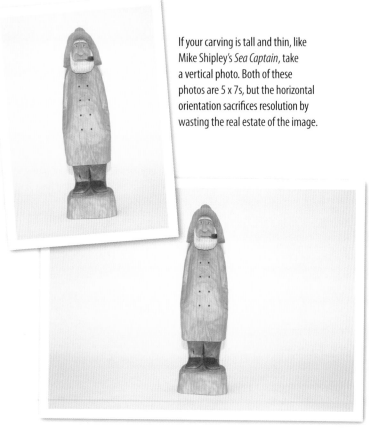

If your carving is tall and thin, like Mike Shipley's *Sea Captain*, take a vertical photo. Both of these photos are 5 x 7s, but the horizontal orientation sacrifices resolution by wasting the real estate of the image.

If you do use a 3-megapixel camera, do not use the camera's zoom function. Just get closer to the project. The zoom function will give you a lower-resolution image.

When you have a digital camera, look up how to shoot the highest-quality photos. You will not be able to store as many photos on your memory card. TIFF files should be close to 5 megabytes in size, and JPEGs should be about 1 megabyte—at the minimum! Take the orientation of the photo into account. If you have a short, wide carving, take a horizontal photo. If your carving is long and thin, take a vertical photo. You want to try to fill as much of your viewfinder with the carving as possible, and still get the entire carving in.

Most cameras convert the photos to JPEG format (.jpg). JPEG files are a standard file most computers can read.

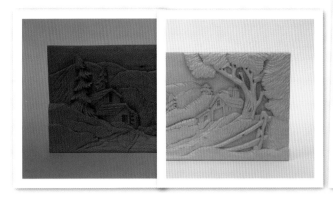

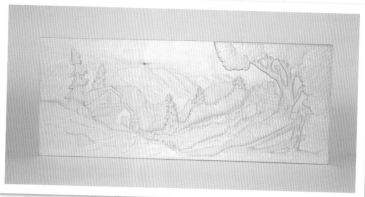

Digital cameras have a "white balance" setting in place to compensate for different lighting conditions. If you choose the wrong setting, the photos will take on an odd color.

Shot with only a camera's on-board flash, the carving looks flat and one-dimensional. If you light a relief carving poorly, it ends up looking more like a line drawing than a carving.

Lighting

One lighting concern is the white balance of the photograph. Natural light, incandescent light, and florescent light each take on a different color. Incandescent light tends to be red-toned, and florescent light tends to have a blue tone. If using a film camera, there isn't much you can do, but most modern digital cameras have a white balance adjustment that will compensate for the lighting.

If something is lighted poorly, the carving either looks one dimensional and flat, or the shadows obscure the carving's details.

It doesn't take professional-grade equipment to do an acceptable job of photographing a carving. Pick up a couple of adjustable desk lamps, fit one with the largest bulb it can handle (usually between 60 and 75 watts), and put a slightly smaller bulb in the second lamp. Get a white sheet or piece of cheesecloth to soften the lights.

Carvings need either a one-light or two-light system. The first light is a fill light. This should never be the camera's on-board flash (too harsh), but an independent light as described above. The fill light should be positioned to light the front of the carving fully, but it shouldn't be strong enough to cast shadows on its own. The other light is the main light. It crosses the subject and casts a few shadows. It may seem odd to add shadows to a photograph, but these controlled shadows add dimension and depth.

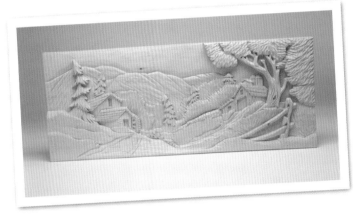

A single soft light source at a hard angle to the subject is the best way to light a relief carving. This photo of a relief carving by Lora S. Irish shows how the main light, properly positioned, highlights the details of the carving and adds the shadows needed to show depth.

Shadows are even more critical for relief carvings. The point of a relief carving is to cast shadows in different parts to create the illusion of depth.

For the photo above, the main light was positioned over and in front of the carving to cast the appropriate shadows into the undercut areas. If the shadows are too dark, you need more light. Hold a piece of white poster board at an angle to bounce more light into the deep areas.

You do not want a fill light when photographing a relief carving. It is very difficult to position the main light and the fill light so the fill light doesn't overpower the main light. If the fill light does overpower the main, the relief carving looks more like a line drawing. That problem is compounded by the light-colored wood used in this carving. The strong flash glared off the light wood and washed away the details of the carving.

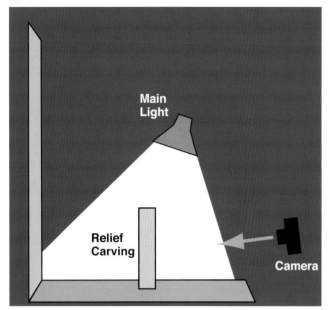

A one-light setup provides the dramatic high-angle lighting needed to properly illuminate a relief carving.

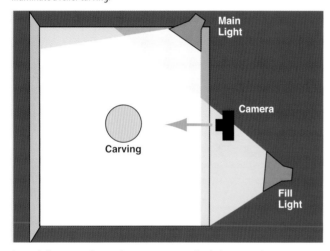

A two-light setup is the simplest way to give quality lighting to a three-dimensional subject. A crossing main light will cast defining shadows, while a soft fill light will prevent the shadow areas from losing detail.

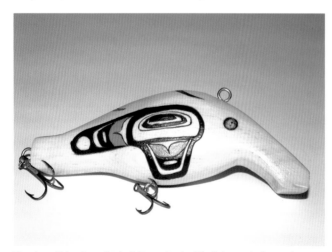

The glare off the glossy finish of this carving by Alfie Fishgap is bad enough to obscure the painting details.

The lighting techniques change when photographing a carving in the round. Use both the main light and the fill light to capture the depth. Set the main light so it shines on the carving from slightly above. It should shine across the carving—highlighting some parts and shadowing others. The fill light should shine across the entire piece. It sometimes helps to shift the pose of the carving to highlight details, instead of shooting straight on.

The last lighting concern is glare. The usual culprit for producing excessive glare is the camera's own on-board flash. Many carvings have a glossy finish, and if the finish is glossy enough to reflect ordinary light, the bright light of a flash will appear as a glare to the camera.

Override the camera's flash unit when shooting any glossy subject. If you are not using a flash and glare is still a problem, change the angle of your main light or the subject itself, as it is most likely reflecting light directly into the camera lens. Also, check to see that your fill light is not too strong.

Focus

Most people have what are called "point and click" cameras with an auto focus feature. No one wants to fiddle around with a lens to try to get something into focus. But auto focus cameras tend to pick one spot on the piece and focus on that specific part, throwing the rest out of focus.

For the most part, cameras have difficulty focusing on a subject when you are very close to it or using the zoom function. If pulling back doesn't help the camera focus, hold a $1 bill in the center of the carving—where you want the camera to focus—until the camera's auto focus locks in. Remove the bill and snap the photo.

Background

A good background doesn't draw the eye away from the carving. The carving should be the focal point. The texture and lighting should focus on the carving. It is important to think about what is behind your carving when snapping a photo.

A good background makes the carving stand out. That means, for a light carving, choose a dark background. A dark carving shows up best against a light background.

Also, try to pick a plain background. Poster board, a bed sheet, a canvas dropcloth, or some sort of fabric all work well. If you are using fabric, be sure it is clean and free of folds or wrinkles. A roll of photo background paper is your best bet and can be picked up at a photo supply store. Make sure paper backdrops do not have tears or creases. Avoid putting the carving on a piece of carpet—the camera will pick up any color variation in the carpet, and the carpet's weave will distract the eye.

If you are photographing a carving in place—whether it is a large carving that can't be moved, or a carving you'd prefer to shoot in a rustic setting—take a look at what is around it. When shooting outdoors, pay attention to parked cars, power lines, chain-link fences—anything that will distract from your subject. If you want to photograph your carving in the shop, try throwing some cloth over your extra tools or move the carving to the least busy part.

Whatever you choose as a background for your carving, make sure the carving is far enough away that your lights don't cast a shadow onto the background. This shadow is almost as distracting as a textured background.

Above all, find a place to photograph your work. Resist using the sofa or kitchen table as a photo studio. If you have room to carve, you have room to shoot.

Plywood Photo Studio

Crosscut a sheet of ¾" plywood into two 4' x 4' sections and join them with three utility hinges along one edge. Set it up on sawhorses and open it up to rest one half against a wall. You now have a portable photo stage that folds flat when not in use, but provides sturdy support for backdrops and carvings when needed. You can cut handles into the plywood to make it easier to carry.

This carving is too close to the background, and the flash is casting a harsh shadow on the background.

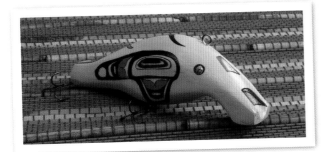

A busy background draws the eye away from the details of a carving.

Not only can textures and color be distracting, but counters, cupboards—and outdoors, cars, and trees—can draw attention away from the carving.

Contributors

Charles Berold
Charles Berold specializes in making custom, diminutive V-tools and veiners.

Andre Breau
Andre Breau is a long-time carver and resident of Canada.

John Brice
John Brice, of Greenleaf, WI, has his own cabinet-making shop. He has been carving for about six years. A wildlife artist, he won the People's Choice award in the Woodcraft/*Woodcarving Illustrated* Wildlife Carving Contest. He enjoys making his own carving tools and accessories.

Charles Brown
Charles Brown of Cincinnati, OH, was the winner of the 2005 *WCI* Poor Man's Tool Contest with his homemade lapboard.

Gene Carey
Gene Carey is a woodcarver from Cicero, NY.

Lori Corbett
Lori Corbett of St. Anthony, ID, is a frequent contributor to *Woodcarving Illustrated* and the author of *Carving Award Winning Songbirds*. She offers several 2½ day workshops a year on color mixing at her studio. For more information, visit Lori's website at *www.WhisperingEagle.com.*

Vernon DePauw
Vernon DePauw started carving in seventh grade shop class and has been carving for pleasure and profit ever since. For more of his work, visit his website at *www.vldwoodcarver.com.*

Lynn Diel
A woodcarver who enjoys designing affordable tools and accessories and a frequent contributor to *WCI*, Lynn Diel lives with his family in Columbia, MO.

Bob Duncan
Bob Duncan is the Technical Editor of *Woodcarving Illustrated*.

Andy Fairchok
Andy Fairchok is a retired IBM software engineer. A carving instructor, writer, and distributor for Kurt Koch books and tools, Andy lives in Prescott Valley, AZ.

Jim Farley
Jim Farley and his wife, Simona DeLuca, live in Europe. Jim is an industrial and systems engineer from Toledo, OH. He caught the woodcarving bug about 5 years ago while living in Italy.

Louis Foshay
A retired machinist who took up carving after attending a craft show in 1998, Louis Foshay was the First Place Winner of the Second Poor Man's Tool Contest.

James M. Haumesser
James M. Haumesser, of Phoenix, AZ, carves carousels and also creates a variety of scrolled and intarsia projects based on carousels. For more of his work, visit *www.creativecarousels.com.*

Joel Hull
Joel Hull is a professional carver and instructor. He has been a Contributing Editor at *Woodcarving Illustrated*. He lives in Port Jefferson, NY.

Lora S. Irish
Lora S. Irish is a nationally known artist and author. Visit her digital pattern warehouse—*www.CarvingPatterns.com*. The website features free patterns and patterns for purchase.

Elmer Jumper
A carver who enjoys turning household items into useful tools and accessories, Elmer Jumper lives in Philadelphia, PA.

Jack Kochan
Primarily a power carver, Jack grinds and refines a variety of subjects in wood from birds to caricatures. Jack is a frequent contributor to and illustrator for *Woodcarving Illustrated*. He lives with his wife June in Reading, PA.

Ed Legg
Ed Legg is a long-time wildfowl carver.

Barbara Marraro
Barbara Marraro is a woodcarver from Boerne, TX.

John Mignone
John Mignone is a woodcarver, classical musician, and a tree propagator. He has carved professionally since 1990, and has been a Contributing Editor at *Woodcarving Illustrated*. John lives in East Meadow, NY.

Richard Rayburn
Richard Rayburn is a woodcarver from Ashland, KY.

Vicki Rhodes
Vicki Rhodes is the author of two books and numerous magazine articles. Contact Vicki at **vrhodes@frontiernet.net.**

Roger Schroeder
Roger Schroeder is a retired teacher, an accomplished author, and was the founding editor for *Woodcarving Illustrated*.

Jim Smith
Jim Smith works as a training and documentation manager. He lives in Madison, WI.

Ernest Szentgyorgyi
Ernest is a professional woodcarver, and was trained in Europe. His business, St. George Euro Designs Corp., specializes in mantles and fine furniture commissions. Check out his website at *www.eurodesignscarving.com.*

Dick Truesdell
Dick Truesdell is a retired electrical engineer who became interested in woodcarving over a decade ago. His early interests focused on songbirds, but after inspirational classes offered by Kirt Curtis and Linda Langenberg, he shifted his attention to animals. Dick lives in Marion, IA.

Mike Way
Mike Way, his wife, and his son live in Surfside Beach, SC, where he tries to keep at least one work in progress and still find time for trips, fishing, and work. A current goal is to create a string of working decoys that will pass as decorative in the off-season.

Melvin Wheatley
Melvin Wheatley, a carver from College Place, WA, was a winner in *WCI*'s Second Poor Man's Tool Contest.

Index

Cover designer: Troy Thorne

Copy editor: Paul Hambke

Designer: Dan Clarke

Developmental editor: Gretchen Bacon

Editorial Assistant: Liz Norris

Project editor: Kerri Landis

Proofreader: Lynda Jo Runkle

Indexer: Jay Krieder

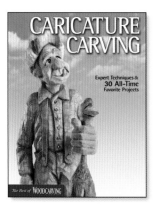
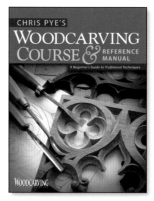
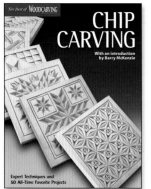
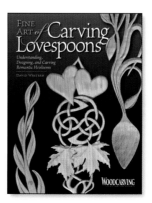
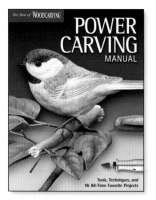
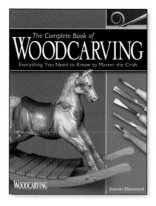
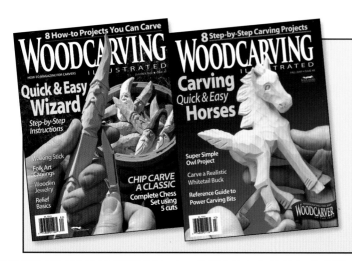